ECO-
IMPERIALISM

ECO-IMPERIALISM

GREEN POWER
BLACK DEATH

www.Eco-Imperialism.com

Paul Driessen

Free Enterprise Press
BELLEVUE, WASHINGTON
Distributed by Merril Press

First Edition
Published by The Free Enterprise Press

Typeset in Times New Roman by Jessica Cantelon for The Free Enterprise
Press, a division of the Center for the Defense of Free Enterprise, 12500
N.E. 10th Place, Bellevue, Washington 98005. Telephone 425-455-5038.
Fax 425-451-3959. Center Website: www.cdfe.org. E-mail address:
books@cdfe.org.

Cover photo by AP/Worldwide, design by Northwoods Studio.

ECO-IMPERIALISM is distributed by Merril Press, P.O. Box 1682,
Bellevue, Washington 98009. Additional copies of this book may be
ordered from Merril Press at $15.00 each. Merril Press Website
:www.merrilpress.com. Phone 425-454-7009.

LIBRARY OF CONGRESS CATALOGING-IN-PUBLICATION DATA
Driessen, Paul, 1948 Jan. 21-
    Eco-Imperialism : green power, black death / Paul Driessen – 1st ed.
    p.   cm.
    Includes bibliographical references and index.
    ISBN 0-939571-23-4
    1. Environmental responsibility. 2. Environmentalism–Social aspects
–Developing countries. 3. Social responsibility of business. 4. Deep
ecology. I. Title.

GE195.7.D75 2003
363.7'0525'091724--dc22

                                                        2003049419

Second printing

PRINTED IN THE UNITED STATES OF AMERICA

CONTENTS

About the Author

Paul Driessen is a senior fellow with the Committee For A Constructive Tomorrow and Center for the Defense of Free Enterprise, and senior policy advisor for the Congress of Racial Equality, nonprofit public policy institutes that focus on energy, the environment, economic development, human rights and international affairs. He speaks regularly about eco-imperialism and related issues on college campuses and radio talk shows and in other forums, in the United States and overseas.

During a 25-year career that included staff tenures with the United States Senate, Department of the Interior and an energy trade association, he has spoken and written frequently on energy and environmental policy, global climate change, corporate social responsibility and other topics. He's also written articles and professional papers on marine life associated with oil platforms off the coasts of California and Louisiana – and produced a video documentary on the subject.

Driessen received his BA in geology and field ecology from Lawrence University, JD from the University of Denver College of Law, and accreditation in public relations from the Public Relations Society of America. A former member of the Sierra Club and Zero Population Growth, he abandoned their cause when he recognized that the environmental movement had become intolerant in its views, inflexible in its demands, unwilling to recognize our tremendous strides in protecting the environment, and insensitive to the needs of billions of people who lack the food, electricity, safe water, healthcare and other basic necessities that we take for granted.

For more information about Paul Driessen, this book and these issues, you are invited to visit the author's website:

www.Eco-Imperialism.com

Introduction

This book should have been written years ago.

It reveals a dark secret of the ideological environmental movement. The movement imposes the views of mostly wealthy, comfortable Americans and Europeans on mostly poor, desperate Africans, Asians and Latin Americans. It violates these people's most basic human rights, denying them economic opportunities, the chance for better lives, the right to rid their countries of diseases that were vanquished long ago in Europe and the United States.

Even worse, in league with the European Union, United Nations and other bureaucrats, the movement stifles vigorous, responsible debate over energy, pesticides, biotechnology and trade. It prevents needy nations from using the very technologies that developed countries employed to become rich, comfortable and free of disease. And as a consequence, it sends millions of infants, children, men and women to early graves every year.

The ideological environmental movement is a powerful $4-billion-a-year US industry, an $8-billion-a-year international gorilla. Many of its members are intensely eco-centric, and seem to believe that wildlife and ecological values are more important than human progress or even human life.

They have a deep fear and loathing of big business, technology, chemicals, plastics, fossil fuels and biotechnology – and they insist that the rest of world should acknowledge and live according to their fears and ideologies. They are masters at using junk science, scare tactics, intimidation, and bogus economic and health claims to gain even greater power

As this book forcefully points out, these radical activists have now wrapped their ideologies up in several elastic principles that focus on perceived environmental threats and largely ignore human needs: corporate social responsibility, sustainable development, the precautionary principle and socially responsible investing. What makes *Eco-Imperialism* unique, though, is not just its insightful analysis of corporate and environmental "ethics," but its reliance on personal, sometimes angry observations by people from less developed countries, who must bear the brunt of these misguided environmental policies.

The ideological environmentalists are helped every step of the way by people who ought to know better, and ought to be the first to challenge their assumptions, claims and demands: corporate executives, US civil rights leaders, politicians, journalists and even clergy. They should be paying intense attention to the issues raised in this book. Instead, they typically ignore them, preferring to focus on alleged misdeeds of their political opponents, perceived slights, exaggerated risks and other contrived problems. By their silence, they accept and encourage the human rights violations, and the brutalizing of entire nations and continents.

During the 2003 World Trade Organization meeting in Cancun, Mexico, the Congress of Racial Equality confronted a number of extremist environmental groups with these facts. We discovered that they were very uncomfortable with having to defend the indefensible – as well they should be. CORE concluded that the time has come to hold these radicals to civilized standards of behavior, end the tolerance for their lethal policies, and demand that they be held accountable for their excesses and the poverty, disease and death they have perpetrated on the poor and powerless. *Eco-Imperialism* begins to do exactly that.

Driessen does a masterful job of stripping away the radicals' mantle of virtue, dissecting their bogus claims and holding them to the moral and ethical standards they have long demanded for everyone except themselves. And he does so with humor, outrage and passion – and always without pulling any punches. Every concerned citizen and policy maker should read this book. Many environmentalists will hate it. The world's destitute masses will love it. And everyone will be challenged by it to reexamine their beliefs and the environmental establishment's claims.

Niger Innis
Congress of Racial Equality
New York City

Author's Preface

The seeds that became this book were planted nearly a decade ago. My work as a senior fellow for the Atlas Economic Research Foundation, an international charitable foundation and public policy think tank in the Washington, DC area, brought me into close contact with people from throughout the Third World. They were engaging, bright, and eager to tell me of their peoples' plight. They have helped me put a human face on my research into the impact of inflexible environmentalism on the developing world. Their courage in the face of overwhelming odds inspired me to take their story to a wider audience.

Like most books, *Eco-Imperialism* is the work of many hands. It is impossible to acknowledge everyone who has shaped my thinking, but a few deserve special thanks.

My gratitude for research assistance and manuscript review goes to Dennis Avery of the Hudson Institute's Center for Global Food Issues, Roger Bate and Richard Tren of Africa Fighting Malaria, Cyril Boynes, Jr. at the Congress of Racial Equality (CORE), Greg Conko and Chris Horner of the Competitive Enterprise Institute, Tom DeGregori at the University of Houston, Barun Mitra of India's Liberty Institute, Julian Morris of the International Policy Network, David Riggs of the Capital Research Center, Professor Don Roberts at the Uniformed Services University of Health Sciences, James Shikwati of Kenya's Inter Region Economic Network. This book would not have been possible without their patience, experience and wisdom.

My thanks for advice, support and encouragement go to friend and colleague Niger Innis of CORE, who also wrote the introduction; Rabbi Daniel Lapin of Toward Tradition; and many others – you know who you are and you have my gratitude – in the global network of advocates for progress and opportunity in less developed countries.

My special thanks, of course, go to my wife Dvorah and children Ari and Amy, who had to put up with the long hours and single-minded effort that this project often required.

The website that is an integral part of the book project was the result of Ari's special talents as a website designer. He created and continues to update the site devoted to this book and the issues it raises at www.Eco-Imperialism.com.

My thanks also to Alan Gottlieb, president of the Center for the Defense of Free Enterprise, for accepting the manuscript for publication by the Center's Free Enterprise Press. More thanks go to Ron Arnold, editor-in-chief, for guiding the book through the production process.

Any merits of this book belong to these fine people. Any errors of fact or judgment are mine alone.

Paul Driessen
Fairfax, VA

Eco-Imperialism

Eco-Imperialism

1

Corporate Social Irresponsibility

UK-based British Petroleum became the world's second largest hydrocarbons producer in 1998, when it finalized a $55 billion merger with Amoco Corporation and changed its name to BP Amoco. After a $36 billion merger with Arco the following year, the company adopted the simpler moniker, BP.

Now, however, say corporate marketing campaigns, BP no longer stands for British Petroleum, but for *Beyond* Petroleum.[1]

The company installed expensive solar panels on 200 of its 17,000 service stations and, over a two-year period, spent nearly $200 million on a barrage of clever news releases and newspaper, television and "wall" ads on the sides of buildings. All carried the same basic messages: We protect the environment, vigorously support the Kyoto global warming treaty, and devote vast sums to wind and solar energy. By the way, we still produce petroleum. (But we produce it more responsibly than our competitors).

Television and print "interviews" with people on the street expanded on the same themes. One "Great Beyondo" ad announced that BP was the first oil company to publicly recognize the risks of global climate change and set a target to reduce its own greenhouse gas emissions. Another claimed the company had voluntarily introduced cleaner burning low-sulfur fuels. Yet another said, "We're one of the largest producers of natural gas ... and are investing in the new energy sources of the future – hydrogen and wind. It's a start."

An enormous wall ad in Washington, DC boldly proclaimed: "Solar, natural gas, hydrogen, wind. And oh yes, oil. It's a start." Another tried to get this line beyond the guffaw test: "We believe in alternative energy. Like solar cappuccino."

The ads did not go unchallenged, however. Conservatives, environmentalists and journalists alike voiced bemusement, skepticism and even outrage. More than one critic suggested that the credibility of the Beyond Petroleum message was neatly summed up by the fact that the enormous (30 x 60 foot) "wall" ads were made of vinyl – as in plastic, as in petroleum.

Certainly, the ads stretched the truth, glossed over inconvenient facts, and relied more on spin than on science, economics or reality. Charitable critics called it "puffery" – grandiose claims that most consumers would not accept as factual. Others weren't so kind.

A major business magazine harrumphed: "Well, please: If the world's second largest oil company is beyond petroleum, *FORTUNE* is beyond words."[2] Several commentators noted that BP's total six-year, $200-million investment in renewable technologies was the same amount it spent in two years on its "Beyond Petroleum" ad campaign – or a mere 0.2 percent of what it spent to buy Arco and Amoco.

Dutch activists decried the corporate campaign as "hypocrisy," suggested that BP actually stands for "Boiling the Planet," and noted that "the company is still increasing oil production ... and moving to exploit some of the world's most sensitive ecological areas."[3] Others derided the entire campaign as blatant "greenwashing" – disinformation intended to present an environmentally responsible public image. BP, they said, is hardly beyond petroleum; it's "all about petroleum."[4] One wag even suggested that BP might want to address its identity crisis yet again, file for one more name change – and just call the company BS.

To cap it off, just as the ad campaign was winding down, BP announced it was spending $6.75 billion for a 50 percent controlling interest in a rich Russian oil prospect – and would be spending an additional $20 billion over the next five years exploring this and other newer fields around the world. Those investment decisions reflect the fact that chief executive Lord John Browne had been forced to lower BP's petroleum production estimates three times in late 2002, leaving investors less than pleased with the company's relatively poor return on capital, especially compared to archrivals ExxonMobil and Royal Dutch/Shell.

So, if BP ever really was Beyond Petroleum, the company is now definitely going *Back* to Petroleum, in hopes that doing so will generate Bigger Profits.

However, much more is involved here than simple puffery, hypocrisy or greenwashing. The advertising campaign also reflects BP's Herculean efforts to lend continued legitimacy to its deep involvement in a movement that purports to judge corporate activities according to a new set of ethical and behavioral standards.

Corporate social responsibility (CSR) argues that companies must not conduct their affairs merely to further corporate goals and earn profits for their shareholders – or even just to provide products and services that meet consumer needs and enrich people's lives. They must also further the "well-being of society" and meet "society's expectations," by "reaching out" to the broader communities in which they operate. They need to "give something back" to the societies that grant them corporate charters and licenses to operate.

The basic concept of corporate social responsibility is "not something that was invented yesterday," says Sir Robert Wilson, chairman of the Rio Tinto mining company. "To many it was simply known as good corporate citizenship, and was founded in treating employees, customers and suppliers with respect and integrity, and taking all due care to minimize harm to the environment."[5] Achieving these goals rarely comes easily, he submits, but depends on a deep corporate commitment to outreach, shared values and mutual trust. In an era of global enterprises, this commitment must often extend far beyond the home borders, into territories and cultures of distant lands and primitive, indigenous peoples.

Even Adam Smith's 1776 classic *The Wealth of Nations* alluded to an expectation that businesses would ultimately serve society. "An invisible hand," he argued, leads a business owner "to promote an end, which was no part of his intention. By pursuing his own interest, he frequently promotes that of the society more effectually than when he really intends to promote it." In pursuing "his own gain," Smith reasoned, the business owner must also meet the needs, desires and expectations of his customers and community, or he will not long remain in business.

In an era of "robber barons," rampant pollution, "company stores" and child labor, Milton Hershey was notable for his benevolence toward orphans and employees alike, as well as for his fine chocolates. Even Andrew Carnegie and John D. Rockefeller – having spent their lives building empires and, at times, abusing employees and driving competitors into oblivion – devoted their retirement years and fortunes to performing good deeds and endowing worthwhile causes to rehabilitate their reputations.

Although scurrilous tales of corporate greed and evil still dominate page one headlines and Hollywood movie scripts, most companies have long been good corporate citizens. At the very least, they scrupulously obeyed the laws and supported families and institutions in their communities. Over the years, many came to realize that their actions can generate significant social, economic and environmental effects at the local, regional or international level, and that they need to emphasize long term responsibility and responsiveness over short term profits.

In the 1960s, a more formalized notion of corporate social responsibility began to take shape in the writings of Howard Bowen, Joseph McGuire and others. They proposed that companies should have even broader visions, be more responsive to needs and issues external to the corporation and its shareholders, and respond still more effectively to outside constituents via formalized community relations and outreach.[6]

Over the coming years, Robert Freeman spearheaded discussions of "stakeholder" involvement in strategic management. He defined a stakeholder as "any group or individual who can affect or is affected by the achievement of the organization's objective."[7]

Initially, the stakeholder concept centered on people in communities that were most directly affected by decisions that lead to employment or layoffs, production or pollution. However, many outside groups also have passionate expectations about what a company does, Freeman and other commentators pointed out – and believe they have a right to influence its direction and decisions, even though they have no legal ownership rights in the corporation.

The list of groups asserting rights to influence society's institutions thus expanded steadily to include civil rights, consumer, environmental and other groups. In many cases, they claimed "standing" or entitlement to intercede, even though their only "stake" in an issue was philosophical and they were located or headquartered hundreds or thousands of miles away from the corporate offices or activities. The list of issues likewise grew almost exponentially, to include – not just pollution or energy conservation – but also complex new concepts like sustainable development, the precautionary principle, environmental justice, child labor in impoverished Third World nations, and "socially responsible investing."

"This unprecedented explosion of would-be stakeholders created for all organizations an enormous dilemma: how to respond in good faith to the claims these groups were making, without fragmenting in all directions the traditional visions that the organizations had been pursuing," Allan Cohen noted in *The Portable MBA in Management*. "The ongoing accommodation continues to this day, for we have truly become a global 'entitlement society,' in which there is no way to predict who will define themselves as stakeholders and what claims, legitimate or not, they will assert."[8]

Meanwhile, at the international level, a lengthy series of conferences, summits and reports proclaimed the need for urgent action to prevent "imminent planetary catastrophe" from chemical and pesticide pollution, over-population, resource depletion and global warming. The Club of Rome's 1972 *Limits to Growth* report, the Brundtland Committee's 1987 study *Our Common Future*, the *Agenda 21* action plan, and major summits in Rio de Janeiro, Brussels, Kyoto and Johannesburg led to declarations, commitments and treaties on these and a host of other issues.[9]

They also resulted in the formulation of far-reaching policy pronouncements, on what today are inextricably linked doctrines of corporate social responsibility, sustainable development and the precautionary principle. The process continues today, with United Nations Secretary General Kofi Annan taking a keen personal interest in the doctrines and actively promoting their widespread implementation, thereby expanding the power and influence of the UN.[10]

To confront the growing dilemma, regain a measure of control over their core mission, and reach out more effectively to the growing array of stakeholders, a number of multinational companies from 30 countries organized the World Business Council for Sustainable Development. The Council's membership includes AT&T, BP, Ford, General Motors, Mitsubishi, Monsanto, Nestle, Procter and Gamble, Rio Tinto, Shell, Sony and Toyota.[11] By developing mission statements and articulating corporate goals and a commitment to various CSR benchmarks, the companies say, they will be able to meet societal expectations more consistently.

Of course, most modern companies now accept these principles as basic components of their corporate philosophy, whether or not they are members of the WBCSD. They understand that, today, everyone expects to be treated fairly, and enjoy a better world for themselves, their children and their communities. Employees, executives, shareholders, customers and other stakeholders expect companies to safeguard environmental values and human health, root out corruption, conserve energy and mineral resources, minimize pollution, provide jobs, and aid the world's poor. And they expect companies to do all this while simultaneously advancing science, developing new products and technologies, bolstering their competitive positions and profit margins, and meeting the unique needs of the customers, cultures and communities they serve.

But despite the companies' best efforts, the corporate dilemma has only worsened. Activists frequently allege that many companies sign CSR pledges only to garner favorable press, enhance their reputations, deflect criticism or appease their critics. Other businesses, they say, merely hope to delay or forestall new regulatory initiatives, get accolades from "socially responsible investor" groups, gain an advantage over competitors, or generate material for slick advertising campaigns. They give lip service to social responsibility, sustainable development and precautionary principles, activists say, "but otherwise it's just business as usual."

One corporate accountability director aptly summarized it this way. The activists claim "business is out to maximize short-term profit, no matter what. Any corporate protestations of social responsibility are exactly that, they allege – no more than protestations, PR spin dressed up as global citizenship."[12]

The charges certainly resonate in the court of public opinion. BP's efforts to reinvent itself as a born-again savior of the environment, while expanding its core petroleum business to shore up shaky 2002 financial returns, help to buttress the allegations. The actions of many other companies likewise do little to alter negative perceptions.

As Kermit the Frog realized, it's not easy being green. Couched as the concepts are in noble terms of creating a better world, preserving finite resources, and building a "sustainable future," few companies are willing to challenge them, at least publicly. To argue against corporate social responsibility, suggests Gary Johns, director of the Non-Government Organization Project for Australia's Institute of Public Affairs, "is to be a rapacious capitalist."[13]

However, the real root of the problem is far different from what activists allege. The awkward truth is that corporate social responsibility doctrines – as currently defined, interpreted and applied by activist stakeholders, regulators, courts, foundations and international bodies – create significant problems. And not just for corporations. Families, communities and nations, especially in the Third World, are particularly hard-hit.

In too many instances, it is the activists who insist on defining "society's expectations," the "well-being of society," and what it is that must be "given back" to society. Year after year, the demands ratchet upward. And year after year, instead of challenging the activists and their doctrines, many companies attempt to "go along to get along," assuming they can simply pass on to consumers and taxpayers the costs of kowtowing to radicals.

As *The Economist* has put it, they neglect to take issue even with the "nonsensical claims" made against them. They "fall all over themselves to compete for an ethical Oscar." They lumber into the trap of implicitly agreeing with their critics "that companies are inherently immoral unless they demonstrate that they are the opposite – in effect, guilty until proven innocent."[14]

In short they attempt to play the CSR game so as to placate their implacable foes, forgetting Winston Churchill's famous admonition: "An appeaser is one who feeds a crocodile, hoping it will eat him last."

Competing for top honors on various social responsibility honor rolls, continues *The Economist*, "may keep activists off a company's back," at least for a time. "But although sucking up to politically correct lobbyists might seem a small price to pay to keep them quiet, in reality it can reinforce the conviction that companies have a case to answer – escalating criticism, and perhaps helping to create a climate in which heavy regulation becomes politically acceptable."[15]

Other corporations, and many developing countries, take a different tack. They try to redefine the term to fit their own particular circumstances or promote elements of the public interest that they believe are especially important. While some of these efforts have succeeded, many have failed. CSR proponents bristle at such dissent, while continuing their pursuit of increasingly complex and inflexible rules and standards.

In some instances, corporate CEOs and executives cave in to pressure for a totally different reason: to shield themselves and their families from repeated intimidation, and even physical assaults. The militants' repertoire of "persuasive" methods now includes fire-bombings, beatings with pick-axe handles and other methods that a mafia don would certainly appreciate.[16]

Some companies, however, seek less salutary ends, succumbing to the Dark Side of the CSR Force. Indeed, BP's actions may be merely among the more highly visible examples of a propensity increasingly shared by for- and not-for-profit corporations alike:

> to stretch the truth ... reinvent reality ... substitute hype, spin and clever advertising for honesty ... and play fast and loose with ethics, the law and the numbers – in order to promote products and programs, attract investors (or donors), and convince journalists, politicians, judges and regulators to turn corporate and activist agendas into coercive public policies.

Certain activist groups in particular have become amazingly ingenious in promoting their agendas, by cloaking them in the mantle of "the public interest" or "social responsibility." In doing so, many take advantage of the fact that they are not held to the same ethical standards, or covered by the same laws and regulations, that apply to for-profit companies. They behave as though they should not be held accountable for breaches of trust or for the consequences of their actions, because they are "guardians of the public interest," or are too vital to their local (or even the world) community to be "restricted" by rules that govern for-profit organizations.

Even The Nature Conservancy, arguably one of the more moderate and respected environmental organizations, has been roundly criticized for being no more open, honest, transparent or accountable than Morgan Stanley, Enron, BP, Phillip Morris, ExxonMobil or any of the other major corporations that are always in some regulator's or activist's crosshairs. A series of *Washington Post* articles by David Ottaway and Joe Stephens revealed a longstanding pattern of abuses, costly screw-ups (including drilling for natural gas on someone else's property), sales of ecologically sensitive land to its trustees as home sites, and glaring lack of transparency and accountability.

Benefiting immensely from an egregious absence of oversight and regulation over nonprofits, the Conservancy rarely volunteers any details on executive compensation, or a listing of its business dealings with trustees, members of its board or their families.[17] All for-profit public corporations are required to provide this information to shareholders and regulators. But nonprofits are exempt. (Ironically, the first article on The Nature Conservancy appeared the very day the *Post's* business section led off with a story titled "A Crisis of Trust on Wall Street.")

How did this $700-million-a-year organization respond to the criticism, and suggestions that congressional committees might at long last examine the practices of environmental nonprofits? According to TNC's own internal memos, instead of promising reforms, the Conservancy hired outside lawyers and PR flacks to coordinate a damage-control strategy that included expensive full-page ads in the *Post* and other papers, meetings on Capitol Hill, third-party letters to newspapers, attempts to "place stories" in the media describing successful conservation projects, and calls to pacify charitable foundations.

Other environmental nonprofits have been accused of abusing their tax-exempt status – meaning that all contributions made to it are tax deductible and, in effect, granting the groups significant tax subsidies. The Alaska Wilderness League, Natural Resources Defense Council, People for the Ethical Treatment of

Animals and Rainforest Action Network are among the groups whose tax status has been challenged via petitions to the Commissioner of the Internal Revenue Service. Among the charges: devoting excessive efforts to lobbying Congress, instead of to educational activities, as specified by the terms of their special tax status; using false and misleading claims in fund-raising appeals; and urging or training members to engage in high-pressure advocacy tactics or unlawful activities. Whether the IRS will actually investigate the allegations, or take any action to end the abuses, remains to be seen.

What all this reveals is a profound and disturbing convergence of ideology, activism, marketing, politics and financial gain, to further radical political agendas. Indeed, a strong case can be made that this is now the *modus operandi* for the huge multinational "ethical" investment groups, foundations and NGOs (Non-Governmental Organizations) that increasingly dominate the global political scene. Many of these pressure groups frequently work hand-in-glove with companies – condemning and shaking them down one day, then accepting secretive contributions or devising joint legislative, regulatory and public relations strategies with them the next.

   Charles Schwab argues that trust in business will be restored only when companies accept three fundamental principles: transparency, disclosure and accountability.[18] There is no reason that these same expectations should not be applied to unelected activist power brokers, like The Nature Conservancy, NRDC, Greenpeace, Friends of the Earth, Amnesty International, or even US, EU and UN bureaucrats, whose taxpayer-funded grants further support the activist organizations.

   Public pressure, occasional media exposure, "watchdog" groups and government regulators have generally had little influence over their actions. In the United States at least, NGOs are exempt from false advertising, transparency and other laws that govern for-profit corporations. And the groups have failed to apply ethical standards to themselves, despite ample precedent set by the legal, accounting, medical, public relations and other professions. As a result, say many critics, the activist NGOs have for too many years had free reign to misrepresent facts, hide their financial dealings, blackmail companies, ignore needs and desires that conflict with their own, and avoid accountability for the adverse consequences of agendas they promote or impose.[19]

The violations, investigations and legislation of 2002 launched a crusade for corporate and Wall Street honesty, to protect the investing public from the likes of Adelphia, Enron, Global Crossing, Tyco, WorldCom and Salomon Smith Barney. The crusade appears to be achieving the desired results, though not as rapidly as some might like.

However, it is now becoming clear that the demand for integrity must also be extended to radical pressure groups, "socially responsible" investor firms and other activists that seek to use public resources and regulatory regimes to impose their worldview and agendas. They, too need to be scrutinized much more closely – and compelled to operate in accord with the same rules that govern the rest of our society.

The time is long overdue for NGOs, activist "stakeholders" and government bureaucrats to do what they demand of business: Adopt internal ethical standards and penalties, and support legislation and regulations that would apply the same ethical rules and standards to them, as now apply to Wall Street, business and professional associations, and for-profit corporations.

In short, the activist groups need to do what the WBCSD suggests all corporations must do: demonstrate that they can "behave ethically and responsibly, in return for the freedoms and opportunities that society bestows" upon them.[20]

Corporate social responsibility can undeniably be an important positive force for good corporate and societal behavior. It is likewise a useful management tool for articulating and adhering to standards and guidelines for every phase of a company's operation.

However, in the hands of misguided or unscrupulous social and environmental activists, trade protectionists, bureaucrats and corporate executives, CSR can be a dangerous virus, a lethal weapon of mass destruction. Because of their growing status and increasing focus on murky but inflexible concepts of precaution and sustainability, CSR doctrines can stop scientific and technological progress, drive small competitors out of business, limit economic opportunities, and serve as an instrument of coercion, economic control, and worse.

Over the past decade, CSR has evolved into policy dictates imposed by pressure groups, courts and regulators to promote ideological agendas, or oppose projects and technological advances that activists view as inconsistent with precautionary, sustainability and eco-utopian goals. It is also behind an intensifying drive for more numerous and detailed regulations and guidelines, over ever more elements of corporate, societal and personal behavior.

"So what now for CSR?" asks Steve Tibbett, director of campaigns for the radical group War on Want. "Corporate Accountability, rather than Corporate Responsibility, is the new game in town. We want to know what the corporations are up to, to figure out what they should and shouldn't do, and hold them to it. Regulation is now firmly on the international agenda. The OECD, EU and UN have all nodded in this direction, and NGOs have rallied round to back moves to make this happen. Progressive business is welcome to help, but it must do so on the basis that social goals, rather than business ones, should have primacy."[21]

Businesses and anyone concerned about innovation, growth and prosperity should take note.

As important as all this is, however, it is actually just a sideshow. "The litmus test," says Britain's CSR minister, Stephen Timms (yes, the UK really does have a CSR minister), "is the impact CSR has on real people in real situations."[22]

In this regard, where it really counts, CSR routinely fails. In far too many cases, the new responsibility-precautionary-sustainability virus snuffs out the hopes, aspirations, rights and even lives of real people, especially millions of people in Third World. As will be seen in subsequent chapters, it is these stakeholders – citizens of poor countries that are only now taking their first steps toward becoming modern, prosperous and healthy – who are most directly and negatively affected by a wide range of policy decisions. And yet, it is their voices, their needs that are most frequently ignored by CSR advocates.

The environmental movement played a vital, pivotal role in changing laws and attitudes about the need to reduce pollution, conserve natural resources, and protect species and habitats. It made people realize that we can, and must, provide for human needs in ways that reduce ecological damage, in technically and economically feasible ways. Had it not been for environmentalists, we would not have been able to achieve our enormous and continuing improvements in air and water quality, wilderness preservation, automotive mileage, and human well-being. Unfortunately, however, as an increasingly radical leadership took control, certain elements of the movement lost their moral compass. Even Greenpeace co-founder Dr. Patrick Moore concluded that they had rejected their original ethical foundations, and had become anti-business, anti-science, anti-technology and anti-human. They were "hijacked," he says, by people who are politically motivated, scientifically illiterate, and ideologically opposed to numerous programs that could benefit mankind.[23]

CSR too began as a valuable tool, to ensure that critical considerations did not "slip through the cracks." However, like the environmental movement and many scientific and technological advances throughout history, it is capable of both good and evil. The course it takes will depend in large part on how wisely companies, courts, politicians, regulators – and moderate nonprofit advocacy groups – proceed from this point forward.

It can only be hoped that they will take a long, hard look at these interrelated "social responsibility" doctrines, and reevaluate what is really in the best interests of employees, customers, shareholders, families and communities across the globe.

Chapter One Footnotes

1. The $200 million, 2-year campaign was crafted by Ogilvy & Mather Worldwide.
2. Cait Murphy, "Is BP Beyond Petroleum? Hardly," *Fortune*, September 30, 2002.
3. "The climate greenwash vanguard: Shell and BP Amoco," Corporate Europe Observatory Issue Briefing (undated).
4. News release, "Don't be fooled by corporate greenwashing: Groups release list of Top 10 Greenwashers of 2000," Earth Day Resources and ecopledge.com, March 28, 2001 (citing BP as "one of the most prominent examples" for its "beyond petroleum" campaign); Kenny Bruno, "Advertising: Greenwash, Inc.," *Sierra* magazine, May 2001. Greenwashing, notes the Tenth Edition of the *Concise Oxford English Dictionary*, is "disinformation disseminated by an organization so as to present an environmentally responsible public image."
5. Robert Wilson, "Corporate Social Responsibility: Putting words into action," speech to the Royal Institute of International Affairs (Chatham House), London, October 16, 2001.
6. See for example, Howard Bowen, *The Social Responsibilities of the Businessman*, (1953), Joseph McGuire, *Business and Society* (1963). See also Sandra Sutherland Rahman, Sandra Waddock, *et al.*, *Unfolding Shareholder Thinking: Theory, responsibility and engagement*, Sheffield, UK: Greenleaf Publishing (2002), and David Henderson, *Misguided Virtue: False notions of corporate responsibility,* London: Institute of Economic Affairs (2001).
7. Robert Freeman, *Strategic Management : A stakeholder approach,* Boston: Pitman Publishing (1984).
8. Allan Cohen, *The Portable MBA in Management: Insights from the experts at the best business schools,* New York: John Wiley & Sons (1993), pages 17-18.
9. *Freedom 21* offers an alternative to *Agenda 21* and UN/NGO sustainable development initiatives. It focuses on free markets, property rights, self-governance and individual liberty. A working draft of this document can be found at www.freedom21.org/alternative.
10. Any further discussion of these historical trends is beyond the scope of this book. However, interested readers can find a wealth of background material on the origins of sustainable development, the precautionary principle, *Agenda 21* and related topics. See for example Wilfred Beckerman, *A Poverty of Reason: Sustainable development and economic growth,*" Oakland, CA: The Independent Institute

(2002); Indur Goklany, *The Precautionary Principle: A critical appraisal of environmental risk assessment*, Washington, DC: Cato Institute (2001); Wybe Th. Douma, "The precautionary principle," The Hague, Netherlands: T.M.C. Asser Institute (1999).

11. A similar organization, the Prince of Wales Business Leaders Forum, is based in Britain. The United Nations Environmental Program and other organizations have also issued detailed statements on sustainability and precaution.

12. Chris Tuppen, BT director of sustainable development and corporate accountability, characterizing what he views as inaccurate criticism of business, in "Some see a beacon of care, others a PR smokescreen," *The Observer*, February 2, 2003.

13. Gary Johns, "Corporate Social Responsibility or Civil Society Regulation?" Institute of Public Affairs, Melbourne, Australia, Hal Clough Lecture for 2002, http://www.ipa.org.au/pubs/Currentissdocs/Clough02.pdf, page 3. See also Gary Johns, "Protocols with NGOs: The Need to Know," Institute of Public Affairs, IPA Backgrounder, Vol. 13/1, 2001.

14. "Irresponsible: Ethical reporting," *The Economist*, November 23, 2002. The article sharply criticized a "triple bottom line" report titled "Trust Us," by the United Nations Environment Program and a consulting group called SustainAbility. The magazine noted that BAA, BP, British Telecom, the Co-Op Bank, Novo Nordisk, Rio Tinto and Shell scored highest on a suspect rating system that suffers from the defects discussed here.

15. *Ibid.*

16. Terrorist acts by the Earth Liberation Front (ELF), Animal Liberation Front (ALF) and other "ethical" groups have included the destruction of crops, laboratories and countless millions of dollars in research. A senior manager for Huntingdon Life Sciences had caustic chemicals sprayed in his face, other employees had their cars firebombed, and the company's managing director was bludgeoned in his own driveway by thugs wielding pick axe handles. An emerging, "non-violent" tactic involves using sirens and bullhorns to awaken an executive's neighborhood at 3 am, plastering the neighborhood with pictures of "mutilated dogs," and the exec's home and office telephone numbers on the Internet, along with a suggestion that people call at any time.

   See also Nick Nichols, *Rules for Corporate Warriors: How to fight and survive attack group shakedowns*, Bellevue, WA: Merril Press (2001), www.cdfe.org/ecoterror, www.ranamuck.org and www.undueinfluence.org

17. David Ottaway and Joe Stephens, "Nonprofit Land Bank Amasses Billions: Charity builds assets on corporate partnerships," *Washington Post*, May 4, 2003 (first of three articles, continuing on May 5 and 6).
18. Charles Schwab, "My investors, my responsibility," *Wall Street Journal*, November 5, 2002.
19. For additional examples of false and deceptive advertising, factual misrepresentation and extortionate activities by activist NGOs, see Nick Nichols, *Rules for Corporate Warriors*.
20. This lofty language is taken from the World Business Council's 1999 interim report on Corporate Social Responsibility. See Henderson, *Misguided Virtue*, page 70.
21. "Some see a beacon of care, others a PR smokescreen," *The Observer*, February 2, 2003. The European Union's Environment Agency, United Nations Environmental Program and United States Environmental Protection Agency are the major driving forces behind these initiatives.
22. *Ibid.* Timms has formal responsibilities for overseeing corporate social responsibility across the country.
23. Patrick Moore, "Hard choices for the environmental movement," *Leadership Quarterly* (1994), reprinted on www.greenspirit.com/key_issues/issues/12/printable.cfm; "The case for biotechnology: Resisting the anti-science, anti-human obstructions of environmentalists," *American Enterprise*, March 2004, pages 24-27;http://www.taemag.com/issues/articleid.17889/article_detail.asp

2

Roots of Eco-Imperialism

Like a mad scientist's experiment gone terribly awry, corporate social responsibility has mutated into a creature radically different from what its original designers envisioned. It now threatens to cause a moral meltdown, to spawn a system in which the most far-fetched worries of healthy, well-fed First World activists routinely dominate business, economic, technological, scientific and health debates – and override critical concerns of sick, malnourished people in poor Third World countries.

This mutant version of corporate social responsibility demands that businesses and nations conduct their affairs in accord with new "ethical" codes that derive from several intertwined doctrines of social and environmental radicalism.

> • **Stakeholder participation** theory asserts that any group that has an interest in, or could arguably be affected by, a corporate decision or the outcome of a public policy debate has a right to pressure the decision makers until they accede to the activists' demands.

19

• **Sustainable development** (SD) says companies must minimize the extraction and use of natural resources, because corporate activities must "meet the needs and aspirations of the present without compromising the ability of future generations to meet their needs."[1]

• **The precautionary principle** (PP) holds that companies should halt any activities that might threaten "human health or the environment," even if no clear cause-and-effect relationship has been established, and even if the potential threat is largely (or entirely) theoretical.[2]

• **Socially responsible investing** (SRI) insists that pension funds and individual investors should purchase shares in companies that have pledged to conform their corporate policies and actions to sustainability, precautionary and responsibility ideologies.[3]

There is a certain allure to these doctrines – reinforced by news stories and reports extolling the concepts and asserting their widespread acceptance. However, neither the terminology nor its constant repetition represents a groundswell of actual public support or obviates fundamental problems with these precepts. The language might sound clear at first blush. But it is highly elastic and can easily be stretched and molded to fit a wide variety of activist claims, causes and agendas.

As a consequence, the doctrines are the subject of deep concern and passionate debate, as thoughtful people struggle to assess the risks posed for corporations, investors, employees, creditors and customers – for scientific, economic and technological advancement – and for people whose hope for a better future depends on ensuring plentiful supplies of affordable electricity, conquering disease and malnutrition, and having unencumbered access to modern technology and greater economic opportunity. As the debate rages, it is becoming increasingly obvious that the doctrines solve few problems and, instead, create a vast multitude of new difficulties.

At their root is the fact that these intertwined CSR doctrines primarily reflect the concerns, preferences and gloomy worldview of a small cadre of politicians, bureaucrats, academics, multinational NGOs and wealthy foundations in affluent developed countries.

These self-appointed guardians of the public weal have little understanding of (and often harbor a deep distaste for) business, capitalism, market economies, technology, global trade, and the vital role of profits in generating innovation and progress.

Yet, it is they who proclaim and implement the criteria by which businesses are to be judged, decide which of society's goals are important, determine whether those goals are being met, and insist that countervailing needs, viewpoints and concerns be relegated to secondary or irrelevant status. In so doing, they seek to impose their worldview and change society in ways, and to degrees, that they have not been able to achieve through popular votes, legislation, treaty or even judicial decisions.

Inherent in the doctrines are several false, pessimistic premises that are at the core of ideological environmentalism. Eco activists erroneously believe, for example, that energy and mineral resources are finite, and are rapidly being exhausted. That activities conducted by corporations, especially large multinational companies, inevitably result in resource depletion, environmental degradation, impaired human and societal health, social harm and imminent planetary disaster. And that it is primarily profits, not societal or consumer needs and desires – and certainly not a desire to serve humanity – that drive corporate decision-making.

In a nutshell, CSR doctrines are rooted too much in animosity toward business and profits, too much in conjectural problems and theoretical needs of future generations – and too little in real, immediate, life-and-death needs of present generations, especially billions of poor rural people in developing countries. The mutant doctrines give radical activists unprecedented leverage to impose the loftiest of developed world standards on companies, communities and nations, while ignoring the needs, priorities and aspirations of people who struggle daily just to survive.

Actually implementing the doctrines requires significant centralized control of land and energy use, economic production and consumption, corporate innovation and initiative, markets, transportation, labor, trade, housing, policy making processes and people's daily lives. Under the activists' agenda, control would be monitored and enforced through United Nations, European Union, US and other government agencies. All this is the antithesis of the private property rights, capitalism, and freedom of nations, communities, companies and individuals to make their own decisions, in accord with their own cultural preferences and personal or societal needs – and thereby generate innovation, prosperity, human health and environmental quality.[4] The ideological version of corporate social responsibility thus stands in direct opposition to the systems that have generated the greatest wealth, opportunities, technological advancements, and health and environmental improvements in history. Its real effect is to cede decision-making to a few; reduce competition, innovation, trade, investment and economic vitality; and thereby impair future social, health and environmental improvements.

According to activist theology, adherence to CSR concepts generates a "triple bottom line" (economic, social and environmental) that companies should meet in judging "true" profitability and citizenship, David Henderson notes in *Misguided Virtue: False notions of corporate responsibility*. Only by measuring their costs, benefits and profits against all three standards can businesses meet "society's expectations," earn their "license to operate," and "give capitalism a human face," claim the activists.[5]

But CSR's supposedly equal emphasis on all three components of the triple bottom line is typically skewed so that environmental considerations trump all others. This happens even where people's lives are put at risk, as in the case of strident activist opposition to pesticides despite widespread malaria, or to biotechnology despite rampant malnutrition and starvation.

Mutant CSR also enables countries to impose "legal" barriers to keep foreign goods out and protect domestic businesses and interests – typically through the use of malleable precautionary and sustainability rules that make it easy to cite far-fetched, unproven health or environmental risks, so as to justify heavy-handed actions.

Stakeholder dialogue, according to the World Business Council for Sustainable Development, is "the essence of corporate social responsibility."[6] However, many of the "stakeholders" who seek "dialogues" are actually well-funded activist groups that assert a "right" to participate in corporate and government decision-making, simply because they have a passionate devotion to their cause.

Some stakeholders are "shareholder activists," who own substantial shares in a company – or just enough to qualify them to introduce resolutions at annual meetings, demanding that a company adopt their positions and agendas on sustainable development, global warming, the precautionary principle or "human rights."[7] Others may be politicians, bureaucrats and other elites in developing countries, whose personal careers and interests are advanced substantially by being aligned with these causes. That the lives of poor people in these countries might thereby be put at greater risk is often only a secondary consideration.

According to the *Boston Globe*, *Sacramento Bee*, Capital Research Center and others, the US environmental movement alone has annual revenues of some $4 billion, primarily as a result of contributions from foundations, corporations, unions, trial lawyers and taxpayer-funded government agencies. The international green movement's budget has been estimated to be well in excess of $8 billion a year.[8]

As a result, well-organized, media-savvy pressure groups have unprecedented power to promote their agendas, define "society's expectations," and influence public perceptions, corporate decisions, and legislative and regulatory initiatives.

In the international arena, they frequently play a prominent role in negotiations, equal to or more dominant than many multinational companies and even some countries, especially Third World nations. Not surprisingly, the NGOs' agendas frequently conflict with and override the most pressing needs and concerns of people who are struggling to overcome widespread poverty and malnutrition, devastating epidemics, and a virtual absence of electricity and economic opportunity.

Corporate social responsibility, argues Gary Johns, can easily become "an assault on the interests and rights of 'real' stakeholders, those who have invested in or are creditors of corporations. It occurs when managers bow to pressure from interests that have no contract with the corporation, whether by way of employment, or supply of goods or services, or through ownership.

"CSR is also an assault on the interests of the electorate. It occurs by undermining the formal democratic consensus as to what constitutes reasonable business behavior. It also occurs when governments grant NGOs such status that it enables them to set themselves up as judges of corporate behavior," or of national decisions on critical health, economic and environmental concerns.[9]

In many cases, the activist groups' cumulative membership might be less than 0.01 percent of a community's or country's population. No one elected them as stakeholders. No plebiscite was held to make their narrow definitions and agendas the arbiter of what is moral or in the broader public interest. No election, adjudication or even United Nations resolution gave them the authority to exclude other stakeholders from debates and decision-making processes – including entire nations and billions of destitute people, who are being denied the benefits of global trade, economic development, abundant affordable energy, and informed use of resources, pesticides and biotechnology.

And yet, the activists define what is responsible, sustainable or sufficiently cautious, often in a way that blocks any development which conflicts with their agendas. That other people might be adversely affected – or the world's most destitute citizens might remain mired in chronic hunger, poverty, disease and despair – enters only superficially into their calculations.

In asserting their demands, they downplay the complex needs and circumstances that confront companies, communities and nations. They ignore the science-based regulatory systems that already protect citizens from actual risks, and raise public fears of far-fetched risks to justify endless delays or outright bans.

Businesses, elected officials and citizens should take a leadership position on these issues, contest the demands of anti-business activists, challenge their motives and dispute their underlying premises. As Johns suggests, they need to "make the NGOs prove their bona fides." They need to "question the extent to which [the activists] represent anyone or anything; question the size of their membership; question the source of their funds; and question their expertise. In other words, question their standing and their legitimacy."[10]

Instead, too many businesses, community leaders and citizens pursue a strategy of appeasement and accommodation, ceding moral authority to unelected NGOs, bureaucrats, "ethical" investor groups and other activists. Some have actually endorsed the activists' demands and collaborated closely with them, despite serious adverse impacts on the world's poor.

As a result, says University of Houston economics professor Thomas DeGregori, developed country activists are often able to co-opt local movements, hijacking them to radical agendas, brushing aside legitimate local concerns, and leaving the indigenous people worse off than before.

When India's impoverished Chipko people initiated a movement to build a road and gain access to Himalayan forest resources, to create a small wood products industry, First World environmentalists took it over. The voices of real local stakeholders were all but silenced, says Australian professor Dr. Haripriya Ragan, and their struggle for resources and development were sacrificed to global environmental concerns. Leading the assault were radical anti-technology activist Vandana Shiva and groups that "tacitly support coercive conservation tactics that weaken local claims to resource access for sustaining livelihoods."[11]

In other cases, "stakeholder involvement" becomes a form of extortion, in which "corporate greed" is replaced by "agenda greed." In 1995, Shell Oil was preparing to sink its Brent Spar offshore oil storage platform in the deep Atlantic, under a permit granted by the UK Environment Ministry. However, Greenpeace launched a vicious and sophisticated $2-million public relations assault that falsely accused the company of planning to dump tons of oil, toxic waste and radioactive material in the ocean. Shell's timid and unimaginative response to the ensuing media nightmare got the company nothing but a bigger black eye, and it was forced to spend a fortune dismantling the platform onshore.

A year later, Greenpeace issued a written apology, effectively admitting that the entire campaign had been a fraud. There had been no oil or wastes on the structure. Of course, the admission got buried in the business pages or obituaries. Flush from their victory, the Rainbow Warriors went on to shake down other companies and promote bogus claims about chemicals, wood products and genetically modified "Frankenfood."

Embarrassed by its stinging defeat, Shell tried to refurbish its reputation and learn from its mistakes. Apparently, the company's execs never actually graduated from the School of Hard Knocks. A few years later, when complaints alone failed to garner enough media attention to embarrass Shell over its alleged "failure to protect Nigeria's Ogoni people," Oxfam and Amnesty International hooked up with radical greens, to hammer the company for complicity in an "environmental catastrophe."

It turned out the catastrophe was caused by tribesmen sabotaging oil pipelines, says Dr. Roger Bate, a visiting fellow with the American Enterprise Insitute, to get gullible journalists to write stories that enabled Ogoni leaders to extort huge monetary settlements from the company. But Shell paid up anyway, in hopes that the problem would go away. Meanwhile, the rights groups and media ignored the racketeering, effectively aiding and abetting the tribal leaders, and setting the stage for future blackmail.[12]

Sustainable development, as defined by environmental activists, focuses too little on fostering sustained economic development, and too much on *restricting* development – typically in the name of protecting the environment. It also reflects their erroneous doctrine that we are rapidly depleting our natural resources and destroying the planet. The putative welfare of "fragile ecosystems" again trumps even the most obvious welfare of people, frequently leading desperate people to wreak havoc on the very ecosystems the activists claim to be protecting.

Leon Louw, executive director of South Africa's Free Market Foundation, refers to sustainable development as "voodoo science." It never asks "sustainable for how long: 10, 200, 1000 a million years? For whom? Advanced people with unknowable future technology, needs and resources? For how long must we conserve so-called 'non-renewables'? Must our descendants, by the same twisted logic, do likewise? Forever?"[13]

Not one person alive at the dawn of the twentieth century could have envisioned the amazing technological feats of that era, its changing raw material needs, or its increasing ability to control pollution. In 1900, coal and wood provided heat. Air pollution and diseases we no longer even hear about killed millions. Telephones, cars and electricity were novelties for the rich. Common folk and freight alike were hauled by horses, which left behind 900,000 tons of manure a year in New York City alone. The Wright brothers still made bicycles. Air conditioners, radios, televisions, plastics, antibiotics, organ transplants and computers could not even be imagined.

Today, the pace of change is exponentially faster than 100 or even 50 years ago. To define sustainability under these conditions is impossible. To suppose that anyone could predict what technologies will exist, what pollutants will be a problem, what fuels and minerals we will need – in what quantities – is to engage in sheer science fiction. Or in the most deceitful public policy scam.

In short, the fundamental problem with "sustainable development," says Oxford University economist Dr. Wilfred Beckerman, is its demand that radical prescriptions be followed to achieve narrowly defined ends, determine which trade-offs should be emphasized, and decide which trade-offs are to be ignored. Here the concept has nothing to add. "Indeed, it subtracts from the objective of maximizing human welfare, because the slogan of sustainable development seems to provide a blanket justification for almost any policy designed to promote almost any ingredient of human welfare, irrespective of its cost and hence irrespective of the other ingredients of welfare."[14]

Precautionary theories likewise promote agendas set by eco-centric activists in developed countries. They ignore countervailing interests and needs of developing nations, such as: creating economic opportunity, ensuring adequate and reliable supplies of affordable energy, alleviating poverty, malnutrition and disease – and ultimately improving environmental quality and ensuring more sustainable practices. It gives CSR, SD and PP precepts credit for any potential public health and environmental risks they might reduce, public policy analyst Indur Goklany points out, but imposes no "discredit" for risks, injuries or deaths that they might generate.

Precautionary doctrines hold that, if anyone raises doubts about the safety of a technology, the technology should be severely restricted, if not banned outright, until it is proven to be absolutely safe. But improved safety resulting from introducing the new technology is typically ignored or given short shrift. The precautionary principle also holds that the more serious the theoretical damages, the more society should spend on precautionary measures, or be willing to sacrifice in opportunities foregone. Moreover, say its proponents, the inability to prove how much society might gain or lose from taking those measures should not stand in the way of extreme caution.[15]

The net result is that the precautionary principle repeatedly stifles risk-taking, innovation, economic growth, scientific and technological progress, freedom of choice, and human betterment. Had it governed scientific and technological progress in past centuries, numerous historic achievements would have been limited or prevented, according to 40 internationally renowned scientists who were surveyed by the techno-whiz-kids at *Spiked*, in advance of its May 2003 London conference, "Panic Attack: Interrogating our obsession with risk."

The experts listed modern marvels from A to Z that the precautionary principle would have stopped dead in their tracks: airplanes, antibiotics, aspirin and automobiles; biotechnology, blood transfusions, CAT scans and the contraceptive pill; electricity, hybrid crops and the Green Revolution; microwaves, open heart surgery and organ transplants; pesticides, radar and refrigeration; telephones, televisions, water purification and x-rays – to name but a few.

Imagine what our lives would be without these technological miracles. As Adam Finn, professor of pediatrics at Bristol University's Institute of Child Health observed, "pretty much everything" would have been prevented or limited under this stifling principle, because "there is nothing we do that has no theoretical risk, and nearly everything carries some risk." [16]

Had today's technophobic zealots been in charge in previous centuries, we would have to roll human progress back to the Middle Ages – and beyond, since even fire, the wheel and organic farming pose risks, and none would have passed the "absolute safety" test the zealots now demand. Putting them in charge now would mean an end to progress in the developed world, and perpetual deprivation and misery for inhabitants of developing nations.

Socially responsible investing (SRI) has become another major driving force behind today's CSR movement, courtesy of a growing coterie of activist pension funds and "ethical" investor advisory firms. They claim to represent people who "want to retire into a clean, civil and safe world." [17] On this basis, pension fund directors pressure CEOs and shareholders to meet "acceptable standards" of precaution, sustainable development, social responsibility and societal expectations.

Now, prevailing notions of corporate social responsibility may bring about a cleaner, safer, more civil world for the activists and pensioners, at least in the short run. But what about for the poorest citizens of Africa, Asia and Latin America? Or even the poorest citizens of the United States, Europe, Canada, Australia and Japan?

As to "societal expectations" – don't African and Asian societies have a right to expect that they will be protected against malaria, malnutrition and dysentery? That they will not be told by rich First World foundations, government agencies and pressure groups how they may or may not respond to lethal threats, including those the developed countries have already eliminated?

To suggest that "socially responsible investors" should have free rein to ignore the conditions and needs of desperate people in the Third World is incomprehensible. But that is often the effect of CSR and SRI policies, as the following chapters demonstrate.

Corporate social responsibility may, as its advocates constantly assert, be based on a noble quest to improve society and safeguard humanity's and our Earth's future. This is a fundamental justification for modern ideological environmentalism. Of course, similar claims were made on behalf of other coercive, central-authority "isms" of the twentieth century.

However, debates over corporate social responsibility, stakeholder involvement, sustainable development, the precautionary principle and socially responsible investing have in far too many instances allowed science and logic to be replaced by pressure tactics, political expediency and a new form of tyranny. In the process, they have left many urgent questions unanswered.

> • Are the asserted risks real? Do the benefits outweigh the risks? Will the radical policy proposals improve poor people's lives – or result in more poverty, misery, disease and death for those most severely and directly affected by the decisions?
> • Why have other stakeholders – such as the rural poor in developing countries – had only a limited role or voice in this process? Why are *their* interests not reflected in CSR and precautionary definitions or applications?
> • Why have some companies, foundations and nations collaborated so closely with NGO and government activists in promoting these mutant concepts?
> • What is the source of the activists' supposed moral and legal authority for determining what is "ethical" or "socially responsible" or in accordance with "society's expectations"? Who elected them "stakeholders," to sit in judgment over what is or is not an "acceptable risk," or what costs, benefits and health or economic priorities must be considered (or ignored) in making this determination?

James Shikwati, director of Kenya's Inter-Regional
Economic Network, raises additional questions that weigh heavily
on the minds of people in his part of the world.

- "Why do Europe's developed countries impose their
environmental ethics on poor countries that are simply trying
to pass through a stage they themselves went through?
- "After taking numerous risks to reach their current
economic and technological status, why do they tell poor
countries to use no energy, and no agricultural or pest-
control technologies that might pose some conceivable risk
of environmental harm?
- "Why do they tell poor countries to follow sustainable
development doctrines that really mean little or no energy
or economic development?"[18]

Most of these questions might be unanswerable. But they
certainly merit careful reflection. For in its most insidious role,
corporate social responsibility – as currently defined and applied –
ignores the legitimate aspirations and needs of people who have
not yet shared the dreams and successes of even lower and middle
income people in the developed world. It should come as no surprise
that the poor people in developing countries increasingly view CSR,
not as a mechanism to improve their lives, but as a virulent kind of
neo-colonialism that many call eco-imperialism.

As corporate executives are frequently reminded, nobody
cares how much you know, until they know how much you care. It
might be appropriate to suggest that ideological environmentalism
should devote as much attention to Third World babies, as it does
to adorable harp seal pups.

Television, email, websites, satellite transmissions and even
old-fashioned newspapers have enabled well-financed activists to
concoct, exaggerate and spread public anxiety over a seemingly
endless parade of theoretical risks. Even for Americans – who live
in the safest nation on earth and are unfazed by traffic and numerous
other dangers that pose far greater risks than those trumpeted by
precautionary propagandists – the constant drumbeat of doom is
hard to ignore.

To suggest that the mutant version of corporate social
responsibility doctrines represent progress, "environmental justice"

or ethical behavior stretches the meaning of those terms beyond the breaking point. In the end, what is truly not sustainable are the human and ecological tolls exacted by the callous policies of radical environmentalism.

Perhaps nowhere is that more apparent than in the arenas of energy, malaria control, malnutrition and trade.

Chapter Two Footnotes

1. See for example, Julian Morris, *Sustainable Development: Promoting progress or perpetuating poverty?* London: Profile Books (2002), especially pages 7-19; Stephen Hayward, "Sustainable development in the balance," American Enterprise Institute, *Environmental Policy Outlook*, August 2002; James Glassman, "Moving on from Sustainability," TechCentralStation.com, August 19, 2002. The World Business Council for Sustainable Development, in its 1999 interim report on Corporate Social Responsibility, states that "CSR is an integral part of sustainable development."
2. See for example, www.safe2use.com/ca-ipm/01-03-30.htm, regarding the Wingspread Statement of January 1998; Henry I. Miller and Gregory Conko, "The Science of Biotechnology Meets the Politics of Global Regulation," *Issues in Science and Technology*, Fall 2000.
3. See for example, the Social Investment Forum website, http://www.socialinvest.org/areas/sriguide
4. See Arnold Kling, "What Causes Prosperity," TechCentralStation.com, December 3, 2002; Marc Morano, "Sustainable development called 'antithesis of human progress," CNSNews.com, September 4, 2002.
5. David Henderson, *Misguided Virtue: False notions of corporate responsibility,* London: Institute of Economic Affairs (2001), pages 15-18. See also Steven Hayward, "The new corporate balance sheet: Black, red – and green," American Enterprise Institute, *Environmental Policy Outlook*, October 2002, http://www.aei.org/epo/epo14483.htm
6. WBCSD, *Corporate Social Responsibility: making good business sense*, Geneva, Switzerland (2000), page 15; discussed in Henderson, *Misguided Virtue*, pages 54-57. Many of the Council's members are businesses that would likely profit (at least in the near term) from legislated carbon dioxide limits, for reasons having to do with their particular products and operations. See below, chapter 8, "Climate Change Riches."
7. For example, as of January 2003, Green Century Balanced Fund (a member of the Coalition for Environmentally Responsible Economies or CERES) owned just 100 shares of Conoco Phillips and 600 shares of BP stock in a portfolio that typically held 50,000 to 2,000,000 shares in "environmentally responsible" companies. But these minuscule holdings enabled the Fund to introduce shareholder resolutions at the BP annual meeting.
8. Scott Allen, "Environmental donors set tone: Activists affected by quest for funds," *Boston Globe*, October 20, 1997; S. Robert Lichter and Stanley Rothman, *Environmental Cancer: A political disease?* Yale University Press, New Haven, CT, 1999; Tom Knudsen, "Fat of

the land: Movement's prosperity comes at a high price," *Sacramento Bee,* April 22, 2001; Robert Lerner and Althea Nagai, *Explorations in Nonprofits,* Washington, DC: Capital Research Center, 2002, http:// www.capitalresearch.org/pubs/pubs.asp?ID=61; James M. Sheehan, *Global Greens: Inside the international environmental establishment,* Washington, DC: Capital Research Center (1998).

9. Gary Johns, "Corporate Social Responsibility or Civil Society Regulation?" page 2.

10. *Ibid.,* page 3.

11. Haripriya Rangan, *Of Myths and Movements: Rewriting Chipko into Himalayan History,* New York: Verso (2000), cited in Thomas R. DeGregori, "Shiva the Destroyer," an assessment of green myths and Third World realities, http://www.butterfliesandwheels.com/ articleprint.php?num=17, the website devoted to "fighting fashionable nonsense." See also Haripriya Rangan, "Romancing the Environment: Popular Environmental Action in Garhwal Himalayas," *In Defense of Livelihood: Comparative Studies on Environmental Action,* John Friedmann and Haripriya Rangan, editors, West Hartford, CT.: Kumarian Press (1993).

12. Roger Bate, "Creeping Activism," www.TechCentralStation.com, April 10, 2003. For additional examples of activist extortion, see Nick Nichols, *Rules for Corporate Warriors: How to fight and survive attack group shakedowns,* Bellevue, WA: Free Enterprise Press (2001).

13. Leon Louw, "Poverty today is truly miraculous," *London Telegraph,* January 9, 2002; revised and reprinted as "The Miracle of Poverty: How to prevent prosperity," *the boss,* April 15, 2003 (a monthly magazine for Asian entrepreneurs, edited by Shalini Wadhwa and published in Katmandu, Nepal: www.theboss.com.np)

14. Wilfred Beckerman, *A Poverty of Reason: Sustainable development and economic growth,"* Oakland, CA: The Independent Institute, 2002, page 7.

15. See Indur Goklany, "Applying the precautionary principle to DDT," 2001, Africa Fighting Malaria, available at http:// www.fightingmalaria.org/ddt_and_pp.pdf; Indur Goklany, *The Precautionary Principle: A critical appraisal of environmental risk assessment,* Washington, DC: Cato Institute (2001).

16. Sandy Starr, "Science, risk and the price of precaution," announcing a conference sponsored by *Spiked,* an independent London-based publication that advocates scientific enlightenment and advancement. The panel included professors, former chief scientists and other experts in astrophysics, biology, chemistry, medicine, pediatrics, toxicology and other disciplines. To view the survey results, see http://www.spiked-online.com/Printable/00000006DD7A.htm

17. Mark Gunther, "Investors of the world, unite! It's up to institutional investors to fix corporate America, says the dean of shareholder activists," *Fortune*, June 24, 2002.
18. James Shikwati, "How Europe is killing Africans, *The Day* (New London, CT), February 3, 2003; see also www.irenkenya.org

3

Cow Dung Forever

"**I** would promote solar and wind for power, not damming more rivers," television actor Ed Begley, Jr. preaches when he stumps for environmental causes. "We've dammed most of the rivers in this country. The two most abundant forms of power on earth are solar and wind, and they're getting cheaper and cheaper.... It's much cheaper for everybody in Africa to have electricity where they need it, on their huts."[1]

His position is doubtless sincere, if misguided. Begley is actively involved in a solar-panels-for-huts aid program. But his views strike many as paternalistic – and worse: a source of perpetual poverty and misery for millions, under the guise of preserving ecological values and traditional lifestyles. Solar panels for huts, and huts forever, seems to be their motto.

Certainly, solar panels on huts are a major improvement over "current" conditions in many areas of Africa, Asia and Latin America. But they are a bandaid approach to the developing world's critical electrical deficiency. They cannot possibly provide sufficient power for anything more than basic necessities, and large-scale photovoltaic electricity is far more expensive than what is produced

by coal, natural gas, nuclear or hydroelectric plants. Wind power
has the same shortcomings.

For impoverished countries where few have access to
electricity, these are not idle considerations.

"Environmentalism, couched in difficult-to-combat superficial
imagery, has taken a sinister turn," suggest professors Michael
Economides and Ronald Oligney. "Now highly politicized, it has a gross
disregard for the [positive] impact that the energy industry has on the
world economy. Using moralistic, yet blatantly dishonest slogans and
pseudo-science, the environmental movement has digressed
dangerously and has replaced some of the most radical movements
for social experimentation of the last century."[2] It has repeatedly used
the alleged threat of global eco-catastrophe to override the wishes of
people who most desperately need energy and progress.

The Third World's poor increasingly want to trade their
huts for modern homes, and enjoy running water, refrigerators,
stoves, electrical lighting and other basic necessities taken for
granted by westerners (and by intellectual and government elites
in their own countries). They want to see their children live past
the age of five, and look forward to even better lives for their
grand kids. They recognize that electricity and energy are *power*
– economic and political power to:

- determine their own destinies;
- build modern schools and industries, to foster better
educational and employment opportunities;
- provide sufficient food to make malnutrition and famine
a distant memory; and
- improve their health and environmental quality, by
powering modern hospitals, water purification and sewage
treatment plants, manufacturing centers, and other facilities
that are commonplace in the developed world.

They resent having their choices dictated by First World
environmental activists, under the guise of sustainable development,
the precautionary principle and corporate social responsibility. As
one Gujarati Indian woman told a television news crew, "We don't
want to be encased like a museum,"[3] in primitive lifestyles so
romanticized by Hollywood and radical greens – and so rife with
desperate poverty, disease, malnutrition and premature death.

They bristle at comments like those Friends of the Earth president Brent Blackwelder piously offered in the same television documentary:

"It's not possible for people to have the material lifestyle of the average American citizen. And that's not necessarily a healthy lifestyle to aspire to. In fact, there are many ways in which we find Americans very unhappy, because they can't spend any time with their families, or with their friends. There's no sense of community anymore. It's a hectic pace. Who would want to wish that on the rest of the world?"[4]

For Blackwelder and other environmental ideologues even to suggest that a "hectic pace" or supposed "lost sense of community" is on par with the ravages endured by impoverished people in India or Africa is incredible. As Kenya's James Shikwati tersely put it: "What gives the developed nations the right to make choices for the poor?"[5]

With a population of 32 million people and average annual income of less than $200 per person, Tanzania is struggling mightily against poverty and unemployment. However, unless it can generate far more electricity than wind and solar can ever provide, much of the country will remain an economic basket case.

Worldwide, in an era when the average EU cow gets $250 in subsidies, nearly 3 billion people live on less than $2.00 a day. Their countries face equally bleak futures without ample electricity.

However, in 2002, over 80,000 delegates from companies, environmental NGOs and government agencies flew into Johannesburg, South Africa, for a World Summit on Sustainable Development. Japan alone brought 500 members in its official delegation.

The summiteers claimed to have come to represent the world's poor and solve their problems. However, they rarely consulted the poor or sought their input. In Johannesburg, they apparently did not even want to *see* Africa's poor in person, be reminded of them too often, or hear about their priorities.

"The world summit was centered in Sandton, an exclusive enclave of high rise towers and fancy hotels, built in recent years to escape crime ridden downtown Joburg," University of Maryland professor Robert Nelson observed. Before the summit, poor street traders were chased out, turning the area into what Leon Louw, director of a Johannesburg think tank, called "a White Group Area with all signs of Africa removed." That these street vendors needed to sell their food and crafts to feed their families seems not to have occurred to summit organizers. Meanwhile, top hotels stocked up on Beluga caviar, champagne oysters, prime beef, salmon and other delicacies, to sate the delegates' epicurean tastes.[6]

The surrealistic scene created a sharp contrast, said Shikwati, "between many developed country NGOs and the people they claim to represent. Wealthy countries want the Earth to be green, the underdeveloped want the Earth fed."

Indeed, the delegates spoke loudly and often on behalf of continued small-scale wind and solar projects in developing countries. They opposed hydroelectric, nuclear and fossil fuel projects, and called for passage of the economy-crippling Kyoto Treaty on global climate change.

Yet today, in Uganda, less than 3 percent of the population has access to electricity. Worldwide, nearly 2 billion people still have no electrical power. In these distant places, far removed from American and European comforts and notice, people have no choice but to rely on wood and dung for fuel.

"The human health, economic, and environmental impact of burning these 'renewable' fuels is immense," says Barun Mitra, president of Liberty Institute of Delhi, India. "Young children and women spend hours each day in the drudgery of collecting firewood or squatting in mud laced with animal feces and urine, to collect, dry and store manure for use in cooking, heat, or light – rather than attending school or engaging in more satisfying or productive economic activity.... The refrigerators, televisions and computers that environmentalists take for granted are not to be seen here."[7]

Citing the precautionary principle and sustainable development, environmentalists worry about air pollution caused by the "unsustainable" burning of fossil fuels, and about "hypothetical, long-run risks of climate change," Mitra notes. But they "conspicuously ignore the real risks that poor people face today," including indoor air pollution caused by burning "renewable biomass fuel."

The World Health Organization says nearly a billion people, primarily women and children, are exposed to severe indoor air pollution every year. WHO links indoor air pollution to some 4 million deaths worldwide each year among infants and children – primarily from respiratory illnesses such as pneumonia and tuberculosis. Biomass fuels also contribute to rampant asthma among women, and lung cancer in women "lucky" enough to survive long enough to get cancer.[8]

In urban areas of developing countries, wood burning by poor families is also a primary cause of outdoor air pollution. For example, the "Asian Brown Cloud," which generated news stories and concerns about health effects a couple weeks prior to the Johannesburg summit, resulted from the burning of politically correct "renewable biomass" fuels like dung, grass and wood.

"The unsustainable cutting of firewood on marginal lands also leads to erosion and environmental degradation," Mitra points out. "Reduced economic productivity, increased human suffering and loss of life, and negative environmental consequences all result from the current reliance on 'renewable' energy." And yet, "European governments, third-world bureaucrats, businesses such as The Body Shop and the European Wind Energy Association, and NGOs such as Greenpeace, have decided that 'renewable energy' and 'clean development' are the future for third world countries."[9]

Wind and solar power will certainly play a role, especially for isolated villages. However, unless fossil fuel and hydroelectric facilities also figure more prominently, affordable, efficient, reliable energy, economic growth, improved quality of life and increasing environmental quality "will remain a dream rather than a reality" for poor people all over the Third World, he stresses.

As Mitra and Shikwati see it, what the developing world really needs is not sustainable development but "sustained development," and an end to the "sustainable poverty" that has plagued these nations for centuries. Environmental pressure groups see matters very differently.

In India's Gujarat Province, the Narmada dam project ground to a halt, because Friends of the Earth and other eco-activists pressured international lending agencies to withdraw their financial support. The dam had to be stopped because it would "change the path of the river, kill little creatures along its banks and uproot tribal people in the area," Lisa Jordan, director of the Bank Information Centre, smugly intoned from the comfort of her modern apartment.[10]

The local "tribal people," however, don't appear to appreciate her intervention. Many deeply resent the green activists' well-orchestrated pressure tactics. One resident angrily called the activists' handiwork "a crime against humanity," because the project would have provided electricity for 5,000 villages; low-cost renewable power for industries and sewage treatment plants, irrigation water for crops; and clean water for 35 million people.[11]

People displaced by the new reservoir would have received new homes and farmland, courtesy of the Indian government. In contrast, Mitra points out, when India created new tiger and wildlife preserves, people were forcibly evicted, given no compensation and told they would be fined, jailed or even shot if they returned or tried to hunt in the preserves. Environmental groups applauded the wildlife set-asides. Few expressed concern about tribal people who had been uprooted.[12]

In Uganda, environmentalist pressure and disinformation likewise halted work on the Bujagali dam. Less than a million Ugandans have access to electricity. Millions still do not have the "luxury" of running water, or even safe drinking water.

Worldwide, millions of people die every year from diarrhea and other waterborne diseases, most of them before age five. Imagine not knowing whether the next glass of water will kill you, and you will gain a better appreciation of what life is like for Third World parents and children.

Instead of turning a faucet handle, women and schoolchildren spend hours every day, often traveling miles each way, to bring water to their families in heavy containers carried on their heads or shoulders. If they live to be 40 years old, their bodies are arthritic and bent from the labor.

Africa's poor "should not be allowed to make the same mistakes the developed world did," American and European activists insist.[13] They should opt for wind turbines, or solar panels on huts. Developing countries mustn't dam up good kayaking rivers or use fossil fuels.

So instead, says Gordon Mwesigye, a senior Kampala official, Uganda's poor will again have their choices dictated to them by developed nations. "People will cut down our trees, because they don't have electricity, and the country will lose its wildlife habitats, as well as the health and economic benefits that abundant electricity brings." Air quality will deteriorate, and the region's ecological balance will be increasingly jeopardized, he adds.[14]

Among the health benefits foregone are water purification and wastewater treatment plants that abundant electricity could help bring to these impoverished areas, where nearly every body of water is poisoned by human and animal waste, and dysentery rates are astronomical. Even in a Ghanian village's hospital, "the water looks like rinse water from a washing machine," says an exasperated former US Treasury Secretary Paul O'Neil, who toured Africa in 2002 with rock star Bono. Aid programs have spent a trillion dollars in Africa over the past 50 years, he notes. "I don't understand why one of life's most important conditions, namely clean water, hasn't been solved."[15]

Clean water could come from wells or reservoirs created to drive hydroelectric generators. But bureaucratic inertia and excuses, coupled with environmentalist intransigence, stymie the projects.

Environmental activists simply return again and again to their favorite theme: Earth-friendly wind and solar power could easily replace nuclear and hydroelectric or fossil fuel generating plants. A World Wildlife Fund "public service" spot, for example, opens on a beautiful landscape. The camera zooms in on a huge power plant. The image turns into jigsaw puzzle pieces, and a little girl removes the piece with the power plant – replacing it with one showing three wind turbines. The message: wind is renewable, and better for the environment.

Reality, however, is somewhat less benign than this disingenuous commercial suggests. It takes quite a bit more than three wind turbines to produce this much electricity. In fact, a new 555-MW gas-fired power plant in California generates more electricity each year (3.5 billion kilowatt-hours at a mere 72 percent of capacity) than does the state's entire forest of 13,000 wind turbines. The power plant occupies less than 15 acres. The 200-foot-tall windmills cover over 100,000 acres, spoiling miles and miles of once-scenic vistas and natural areas.[16]

Wind turbines also make life hazardous for birds. The Audubon Society says "more eagles are killed annually by US wind turbines than were lost in the disastrous Exxon Valdez oil spill."[17] A recent study in northern Spain revealed that a mere 400 wind turbines killed 432 raptors, 671 bats and 6,152 small birds in a single year. People there are beginning to worry that birds migrating from Africa to Europe via the Iberian Peninsula could be devastated if Spain moves ahead with plans to build 10,000 wind turbines.[18] But somehow, in the minds of environmental zealots, wind power is still preferable, still ecologically benign.

The day may come when wind and solar provide much more power than they do today – less than 0.2 percent of the world's energy needs – with far less damage to the environment. Right now, however, these renewable energy sources should be viewed as no more than an interim solution for remote locations that lack electricity.

To block the construction of centralized power projects, as not being "appropriate" or "sustainable," is to condemn billions of people to continued poverty and disease – and millions to premature death.

Environmental activists "romanticize poverty," Mitra says. Then they fly to "eco summits" like the one in Johannesburg, where they "stay in five-star hotels, talking about poverty but not giving options to the people who are actually poor to come out of poverty."[19]

And for this, they are deemed to be "responsible," concerned about the poor, moral and "passionate about the environment."

Chapter Three Footnotes

1. Ed Begley, Jr., discussing environmental issues during Public Relations Society of America teleconference on Hollywood support for environmental causes, October 29, 2002. Gar Smith, editor of the Earth Island Institute's online magazine, *TheEdge*, says Africans would spend too much time watching television, if they had abundant electricity. "If there is going to be electricity, I would like it to be decentralized, small and solar-powered," he commented during the 2002 Earth Summit in Johannesburg. Marc Morano, "Environmentalist laments introduction of electricity," CNSNews.com, August 26, 2002.
2. Michael Economides and Ronald Oligney, *The Color of Oil*, Round Oak Publishing Company (2000), page 141.
3. Unidentified woman, *Against Nature*, Martin Durkin producer, London: Channel 4 Television Corporation (1997). A partial transcript from the program can be found online at www.africa2000.com/INDX/channel4.html
4. *Ibid.* Blackwelder also expressed deep satisfaction that FoE and other environmentalists had succeeded in blocking almost 300 dam projects in the Third World.
5. James Shikwati, "I do not need white NGOs to speak for me," IREN Newsletter, September 3, 2002; www.iren.org
6. Robert Nelson, "Partying in Joburg: All told, the Joburg summit cost at least $250 million," Frontier Centre for Public Policy, October 23, 2002.
7. Barun Mitra (Liberty Institute, New Delhi, India), "Stop energy eco-imperialism," PolicyNetwork.net, November 5, 2002.
8. Thomas DeGregori, *Bountiful Harvest: Technology, food safety and the environment*, Washington, DC: Cato Institute, 2002, page 130, citing WHO reports; Douglas Barnes, et al, "Tackling the Rural Energy Problem in Developing Countries," *Finance & Development*, 34(2), pages 11-15 (1997).
9. Barun Mitra, "Stop energy eco-imperialism."
10. *Against Nature*, Martin Durkin producer.
11. *Ibid.*
12. Barun Mitra, Liberty Institute, personal communication with Paul Driessen, November 9, 1999.
13. James Shikwati, "I do not need white NGOs to speak for me."
14. Gordon Mwesigye, discussion with Cyril Boynes, Jr., director of international projects, Congress of Racial Equality, December 3, 2002.
15. "Paul O'Neill's last challenge," editorial, *Washington Times*, December 12, 2002.

16. Ronald Bailey, *Global Warming and Other Eco-Myths: How the environmental movement uses false science to scare us to death*, Washington, DC: Competitive Enterprise Institute (2002), page 250-258.
17. *National Review, The Week*, October 11, 1999.
18. Dr. J. M. Lekuona, report on birds killed by 400 wind turbines in northern Spain, Department of the Environment, Navarra, Spain, 2002 (cited at http://www.darrylmueller.com/navarra_spain_birdkills.html). The report was suppressed by the department and was obtained by a local citizens association, following pressure on the minister.
19. "Protesters March Against 'Sustainable-Poverty,'" CNSNews.com and townhall.com, September 1, 2002.

4

Playing Games with Starving People

Green activists and European bureaucrats may not be conspiring to starve millions of sub-Saharan Africans, but they may as well be, Andrew Natsios charged in August 2002. The director of the US Agency for International Development accused environmental groups of endangering the lives of 14 million people who face starvation in southern Africa, which is enduring its worst drought in a decade, by encouraging governments to reject genetically modified US food aid.

"They can play these games with Europeans, who have full stomachs, but it is revolting and despicable to see them do so when the lives of Africans are at stake," he said.[1] US Trade Representative Robert Zoellick also excoriated European Union officials, calling them "Luddites" and saying it is "immoral" for them to bully Africa into refusing to accept American food shipments.[2]

Nearly 2.5 million people were on the verge of starvation in Zambia alone, where President Levy Mwanawasa bowed to NGO pressure and EU import policies, and refused to accept food aid from the United States.

The US had shipped 26,000 tons of corn to Zambia, where many people were down to one small meal per day, only to have the grain sit in storage. Parroting the EU/Greenpeace line, Mwanawasa decreed it was unsafe for consumption, because some of the corn (maize) had been genetically modified, to make it resistant to insect pests, reduce the need for pesticides, and increase crop yields without having to put more land under cultivation.

"We would rather starve than get something toxic," Mwanawasa cavalierly remarked. Anonymous European Commission officials went so far as to accuse the US of using Africans as guinea pigs, to prove biotech foods are safe to eat. Rumors circulated among the locals that women would become sterile and people would get AIDS, if they ate the corn.[3]

The fact that Americans have been consuming this corn for years did not change Mwanawasa's position. (Over 34 percent of all US corn and 78 percent of its soybeans are genetically modified, as are many other crops.) Nor was he swayed by repeated scientific studies concluding that biotech foods are safe to eat – or by the demands of his own starving people, who on several occasions attempted to break into the warehouses.

The intense opposition to the use of genetically modified (GM) crops as food aid is yet another example of the precautionary principle run amok. Better safe than sorry. Better dead than fed. We had to starve them in order to save them. Said the *Wall Street Journal*:

> "The green brigade, which likes to buttress its political opposition to GM foods with junk science, is cheering Zambia's intransigence. And the willingness of Greenpeace, Friends of the Earth and the like to let Africans starve in the name of someone else's ideology is remarkable enough.
>
> "But the Europeans are also blameworthy. Zambia is just as worried about upsetting trade relations with Europe, its biggest export market. The European Union bans most GM crops – lest they upset Europe's heavily subsidized farm system – and Mr. Mwanawasa's concern is that the US corn will cross-pollinate with non-GM varieties and taint future yields [thus triggering EU bans on crops from Zambia and neighboring countries].

"The eco-lobby has targeted the Third World with a five-year, $175 million campaign against GM foods. The Sierra Club is calling 'for a moratorium on the planting of all genetically engineered crops.' Greenpeace says it "opposes all releases of genetically engineered organisms into the environment," an act it calls 'genetic pollution.'"[4]

$175 million would feed millions of starving people for months. So would the $500 million the protest industry spent between 1996 and 2001 to attack biotechnology. But of course, amply nourished Greenpeace zealots are not spending a dime on food aid. They merely want to scare Africans half to death, if they don't starve to death first.

As for President Mwanawasa and his ruling elites, they are not going hungry, either. Nor are Mr. Mugabe and his cronies in Zimbabwe, who live lavishly on imported European food and luxury goods. They will, however, profit mightily from any agricultural and other trade with EU nations that threaten their countries with sanctions, if the Africans dare to import, export or grow biotech crops. The elites' real fear, in other words, is not "tainted" food – but concern that Euro food fanatics will decree that African crops have been tainted by American GM pollen. Meanwhile, the desperate masses continue to starve.[5]

Indeed, even if malnourished Africans seek to plant disease-resistant GM crops only to feed themselves, the anti-biotech radicals still cry "genetic pollution." And well-fed European countries still threaten to maintain their GM-free-at-any-cost moratorium against the import of grains and other crops from any nation that dares to defy their edicts.

Ugandans eat 500 pounds of bananas per person every year – more than any other people on earth. But their banana crops are being devastated by an airborne fungus that prevents photosynthesis and nematodes that destroy the roots. Scientists have already developed a bio-engineered solution for the fungus, and are hard at work on the nematode problem.

However, implementation of these crop-saving technologies remains snarled in a bureaucratic nightmare that insists Uganda must first construct a legal framework (acceptable to GM-phobic Europeans) to prove beyond any doubt that the non-traditional plant

breeding techniques will not pose any conceivable human health or
environmental risks.

"If I want to eat a biotech banana here, the US shouldn't
care, and Europe shouldn't care," says C.F. Mugoya, associate
executive secretary of Uganda's National Council for Science and
Technology. "If science offers us a solution, we should go for it if
we want." That should be especially true for bananas, which don't
spread pollen and pose no risk of "gene flow" between genetically
engineered and non-engineered plants, which ostensibly is the EU's
concern about GM corn in Zambia and Zimbabwe.

But "if you say 'biotech' here, all hell breaks loose," groans
John Aluma, deputy director general of the country's National
Agricultural Research Organization. Adds W.K. Tushemereirwe,
director of Uganda's banana research program, "The Europeans have
the luxury to delay. They have enough to eat. But we Africans don't."[6]

Many Brazilian farmers are eager to plant herbicide
resistant ("Roundup-Ready") soybeans that allow them to minimize
cultivation for weed control, and thereby reduce soil erosion.
However, legal actions and lobbying by Greenpeace, threats by a
state government eager to sell produce to hyper-cautious European
consumers, and official policies against biotech crops by President
Luiz Inácio Lula da Silva combined to keep Brazil a "GM-free
zone" – until farmers had planted so many tracts of illegal biotech
soybeans that Lula was compelled to relent.[7]

For a long time, Argentina had been the only Latin American
country that enthusiastically embraced biotechnology. That appears
to be changing, even though junk-science roadblocks continue to
thwart its acceptance and use in many countries.

Biotech experts Gregory Conko and Dr. Henry Miller, MD are
blunt in their denunciation of the EU, UN and radical green actions.
This "self-serving involvement in excessive, unscientific
biotechnology regulation," they argue, "will slow agricultural research
and development, promote environmental damage, and bring famine
to millions in developing countries." The UN-sponsored "biosafety
protocol," regulating the international movement of gene-spliced
organisms, is based on a "bogus precautionary principle," which
falsely assumes there are risk-free alternatives, and imposes an
impossible standard on innovation: guilty until proven innocent
beyond a shadow of a doubt.

No longer must regulators demonstrate that a new technology is likely to cause harm. Instead, the innovator must now prove the technology will *not* cause any harm. Worse, "regulatory bodies are free to arbitrarily require any amount and kind of testing they wish…. [T]he biosafety protocol establishes an ill-defined global regulatory process that permits overly risk-averse, incompetent, and corrupt regulators to hide behind the precautionary principle in delaying or deferring approvals," they charge, as in the case of a years-long moratorium on EU approvals of gene-spliced plants.[8]

The principle imposes the ideologies and unfounded phobias of affluent First World activists, to justify severe restrictions on the use of chemicals, pesticides, fossil fuels and biotechnology by Third World people who can least afford the prohibitions. Opposition to biotechnology is "a northern luxury," says Kenyan agronomist Dr. Florence Wambugu. "I appreciate ethical concerns, but anything that doesn't help feed our children is unethical."[9]

Greenpeace co-founder and ecologist Dr. Patrick Moore echoes her sentiments. Now an outspoken critic of the group he once led, he underscores the "huge and realistically potential benefits" that GM crops could bring "for the environment and human health and nutrition." He calls the war on biotechnology and genetically modified organisms (GMOs) "perhaps the most classic case of misguided environmentalism" in memory.

"There are no known serious negative impacts from growing or ingesting the GMOs that have already been developed and distributed," Moore continues. "Yet every half-baked sensationalism and contrivance from activists with no training in science gets airtime on the evening news. Even the Golden Rice, a GMO that may help prevent blindness in half a million children every year, is rejected out of hand by these anti-humanists, who put unfounded fear-mongering ahead of the world's poor."[10]

Anti-biotech activists, in fact, want nothing to do with the precautionary principle, when it means focusing attention on the harmful, even lethal effects that their zero-risk policies and opposition to GM crops impose on millions of people in Africa and Asia. The fact that a quarter of the developing world's children under age ten are malnourished is of little apparent concern to them. They are too busy protesting and destroying potentially life-saving technologies.

Greenpeace and other eco-zealots have repeatedly ripped up experimental fields of GM plants, preventing the very scientific research that they demand as a precondition for issuing permits to grow and market the crops. (Clever, aren't they?) They are also masters of propaganda – using inflammatory terms and faulty science to terrify people and promote their cause. A favorite tactic involves press releases about preliminary studies, to avoid the scientific peer review process and garner front-page *New York Times* and tabloid coverage of studies that are later found to be based on "flawed design, execution and analysis," which in some cases may be a charitable way of saying "fraudulent."[11]

Zealous researchers alleged, for example, that monarch butterflies might be harmed by biotech Bt corn, which contains a bacterium gene (*Bacillus thuringiensis*) that makes the corn toxic to insects that chew on the plants – but harmless to other insects. They also claimed that feeding transgenic potatoes to rats might damage their immune systems. Both "studies" were quickly seized upon by the *Times* and tabloids to generate hysterical reactions. Both were subsequently pilloried by scientific panels.

More careful studies found that the number of monarch butterflies and larvae actually *increased* in fields where Bt corn was grown, probably because the use of pesticides was greatly reduced in those fields. A review of the potato study concluded that the rats' immune systems were damaged largely because they were being fed mostly potatoes, and their diets were severely lacking in essential nutrients.

However, the baseless claims had already influenced many people's perceptions about GM crops, and the activists continue to promote their bogus charges, even today.

The message inside a Mistic fruit drink bottle cap perfectly captures the zealots' strategy: "If you can't be right, be dramatic."

Their abuse of precautionary concepts, to promote their own radical political agendas, never asks the most basic question:

How many children will go blind – how many children, adults and elderly will these radicals condemn to suffering and death – while scientists try to meet the irrational, impossible, ever-shifting standards and approval processes for biotech foods?

Dr. Wambugu spent three years with Monsanto, developing a genetically modified sweet potato that is resistant to a virus that had devastated this important food crop in her native country, leaving hundreds of thousands of children hungry and malnourished. Into the sweet potato she spliced a gene from the pyrethrum, a white flower whose ingredients are fatal to the feathery mottle virus.

This new sweet potato can withstand the virus, "requires no pesticides and holds the promise of feeding some of the 800 million chronically undernourished people in the world," she says. Traditional crops and "organic" farming methods used in developing countries, by contrast, consistently result in low yields and hungry people, especially when droughts and diseases batter the crops.

But as she neared triumph, Earth Liberation Front eco-terrorists destroyed the laboratory and test crops, significantly setting back her life-saving work. What gives these environmental "hooligans" the right to condemn these people to perpetual malnutrition? she wants to know.[12]

Wambugu concedes that GM crops are experimental. However, the potential good far outweighs the risks, she insists – just as penicillin has cured millions of people, while causing allergic reactions in only limited cases. "This is not a question of export to Europe or America," she says. "If they don't want it, they don't have to have it. We have local demand. We're dying. So can we eat first?"[13]

"If today's rich nations decide to stop or turn back the clock, they will still be rich," notes Wellesley College political scientist Robert Paarlberg. "But if we stop the clock for developing countries, they will still be poor and hungry."[14] And thousands, perhaps millions, of their children will die.

What people too often forget is that modern biotechnology is really nothing more than a refinement of genetic manipulation techniques that have been employed for centuries, to create new or improved varieties of flowers, edible plants, cattle and other organisms. Indeed, virtually every plant and animal product we consume today is the result of cross-breeding and other techniques that have been employed for a millennium or more to alter their predecessors' genetic makeup. Even prehistoric farmers selected their best seeds and animals for breeding, to increase size, quantity, quality and yield.

Most people accept that hybrids like these are not entirely natural, because they were guided by human hands. But many still tend to think there is a vast gulf between modification of this sort and genetic engineering. What they don't always realize is that many other advanced breeding methods have been used by scientists to modify plants throughout the twentieth century. As early as 1906, Luther Burbank noted, "We have recently advanced our knowledge of genetics to the point where we can manipulate life in a way never intended by nature."

> • In wide-cross hybridization, for example, researchers intentionally mate plants from different species or different genera that normally are sexually incompatible. This can only be done in a laboratory environment and would never occur in nature. Common examples found in grocery stores include broccoflower (an artificial broccoli-cauliflower hybrid), the tangelo (a cross between tangerine and grapefruit), hybrids of wheat and wild grasses, and fruit varieties like the plumcot (an artificial plum-apricot hybrid).
> • Tissue culture involves taking micro-cuttings from a plant and growing them in a controlled environment to facilitate quick reproduction. Along with this quick regeneration, however, come accidental mutations in the plant's DNA. Most of the mutations are harmful to the plant and are discarded. But some mutations create varieties that ripen faster or are bigger or tastier, but still perfectly safe to eat.
> • Other researchers deliberately induce mutations by bombarding seeds with radiation (or exposing them to chemicals) to create a host of unknown DNA changes that then get passed along in future generations of crops. Over 2,000 of these mutation-bred crops – including varieties of wheat, rice, corn, potato, tomato, and squash – are already sold and consumed every day, all around the world, with no outcry from agricultural purists.

Because all these techniques are considered to be "conventional," sometimes simply because they've been around for several decades, they are totally unregulated. Only rarely are they subjected to the vitriol, legal challenges or import restrictions imposed on GM crops by environmentalists, organic farmers and the EU. Even mutagenic or "mutation-breeding" methods – the least predictable of all these techniques – get a free ride, and their offspring are never branded as "genetically modified" by the food police.

The new gene-splicing methods of biotechnology are simply more precise and predictable than these other methods, and thus yield safer, more predictable products. Today, researchers can select for very specific traits, by introducing pieces of DNA that contain just one or a few well-characterized genes. In contrast, the older genetic techniques bring together or transfer thousands of genes from two or more parent organisms.[15]

Scientists are virtually unanimous about this, and the American Medical Association, the National Academy of Science, and even the Center for Science in the Public Interest (renowned for its attacks on *kung pao* chicken and other foods) have likewise concluded that biotech foods are safe for the public and the environment. More than 3,200 scientists worldwide (including 20 Nobel Prize laureates) have signed a statement supporting biotechnology. Even EU Environment Minister Margot Wallstroem has called the ban on genetically modified crops "illegal and unjustified," and the French Academies of Sciences and Medicine concluded: "there has never been a health problem ... or damage to the environment" associated with biotech crops. Opposition to GM crops, said the Academies, is due to "the propagation of erroneous information."[16]

So it is ironic – and a gross abuse of ethical and precautionary principles – that only the most precisely crafted (GM) crops are tested over and over, and subjected to reams of costly regulations. In the United States, the Environmental Protection Agency examines GM products carefully if they incorporate virus and insect resistant traits. The Food and Drug Administration requires that biotech foods be as safe as conventional foods, and reviews safety testing data for every GM variety that is commercialized. And the Department of Agriculture reviews where any biotech crops will be grown and what effects they might have on nearby environments. Even mutation-bred crops go through no such testing.

"Why should there be different standards for GM crops and pharmaceuticals, particularly in Africa, where the need for food is crucial for survival?" Dr. Wambugu asks.[17] But the excessive testing goes on, at a cost of tens of millions of dollars a year, further delaying the availability of these life-saving technologies.

The delays reflect the radicals' incessant anti-biotechnology campaigns and events that have nothing to do with the safety of gene-splicing techniques.

• GM foods first went on sale in Europe in the spring of 1996, at exactly the moment that "mad cow disease" was finally certified as a human health threat. Mad cow had nothing to do with transgenic crops, but European regulatory authorities had no credibility when they tried to reassure consumers that GMOs were safe, because they had earlier said meat from diseased cows was safe, and had dismissed concerns about AIDS-tainted blood supplies given to hemophiliacs. This and Europe's recent history of Nazi eugenics thus ensured a very receptive audience for radical fear-mongering, and reinforced the tendency of many on the continent to frighten themselves with hobgoblins of their own imagining.

• European resistance to GM foods also reflects their more conservative food culture; more traditional agricultural practices; a strong desire to protect small farmers from outside competition, particularly from US farmers and multinational firms; and resentment of US agricultural, economic, trade and military power.

• The EU's multi-party political systems give radical activists and green parties tremendous influence over regulatory policies, enabling them to exploit public fears.

• Companies like Monsanto and Novartis failed to handle the growing controversy over GM crops nearly as well as they might have., to put it mildly. As a result, the dispute festered and boiled over into the fulsome reactionary climate that confronts the world today.

• In an ironic reminder that attempting to placate radicals is playing with fire, the biotech industry actually lobbied for more regulations during the 1980s and 1990s. Some did so to gain a competitive advantage over smaller rivals. Others simply wanted to be able to tell consumers their products were so heavily regulated that they had to be safe. But now the rules have become so onerous that perfectly safe products are being kept off the market, and good companies have closed their doors, merged or laid off many of their best people.[18]

But why should these facts condemn millions to malnutrition, starvation and disease? That they continue to do so marks another shameful chapter in human history.

By making crops resistant to herbicides, biotechnology also reduces the need for cultivation to eliminate weeds, and thus curbs soil erosion. "Over the past eight years," Robert Zoellick noted in a *Wall Street Journal* column, "biotech cotton and corn have reduced pesticide use by 46 million tons of active ingredients. The Chinese Academy of Sciences estimates that biotech could reduce China's pesticide use by 80 percent."[19] Further advances may soon allow crops to grow in saline soils or be irrigated with brackish water, enable plants to thrive under extreme heat, drought and moisture conditions, and save wildlife habitat by enabling farmers to grow more food on less land.

These qualities are especially important in Africa, where erosion has stripped away fertile topsoil, extremes of moisture, heat and drought are common, and centuries of irrigated farming have depleted soil nutrients and raised concentrations of salts, aluminium and other minerals. All these conditions make agriculture difficult.

Africa missed out on the first "Green Revolution." Pioneered by Iowa farmer and agricultural researcher Dr. Norman Borlaug, this revolution brought new corn varieties to Mexico, new wheat strains to India and new rice to China, saving the lives of perhaps a billion people. Africans can hardly afford to miss out on the biotech green revolution.

As Dr. Borlaug has put it, "There are 6.6 billion people on the planet today. With organic farming we could only feed 4 billion of them. Which 2 billion would volunteer to die?"[20] A more accurate question might be, which 2 billion would Greenpeace, the World Wildlife Fund and the Earth Liberation Front "volunteer" to die?

It is therefore a welcome development that The Rockefeller Foundation and US Agency for International Development have linked up with four of the world's largest agribusiness corporations to launch a new Green Revolution for hungry Africa. As part of the initiative, Monsanto, DuPont, Syngenta, and DowAgrosciences will donate biotech seeds, patent rights, research tools and training in proper laboratory techniques to African scientists, via a new African Agriculture Technology Foundation being established in Kenya, under the guidance of Dr. Eugene Terry. If the rabidly anti-biotech elements can be kept at bay, the initiative could bring real hope to millions.

Assuming it is allowed to take root and flourish, biotechnology is also on its way to transforming corn, soybeans and other crops into little drug factories that generate proteins to combat blindness and diseases that threaten millions of people in developing countries.

Many of the world's poorest people are farm families that subsist on homegrown rice, and sometimes little else. As The Rockefeller Foundation notes, even their infants are fed little but rice gruel, because their families cannot afford meat, fish or even a balanced vegetable diet. However, this rice is low in vitamin A, the rest of their deficient diets do not supply essential vitamins and minerals, and children in rural areas are seldom reached by vitamin A supplementation programs.[21]

The results are tragically predictable and, as always, it is the children who are most vulnerable. According to the World Health Organization, 230 million children are "at risk" for clinical or subclinical Vitamin A Deficiency – and 500,000 children go blind from it every year. VAD also impairs children's intellectual development, and lowers the body's resistance to disease, increasing mortality from malaria, measles, diarrhea and a host of other illnesses. As many as 2 million children die each year from problems directly related to the deficiency.[22]

The new Golden Rice is rich in beta-carotene, which human bodies can convert to vitamin A, thereby reducing these problems dramatically.[23] A mere 200 grams (1.5 ounces) per day is sufficient. But once again, intense opposition by radical groups is generating unfounded public fears and unconscionably delaying efforts to make this miracle technology widely available.

Fungal infestations in vegetables and grains (such as fuminosins and aflatoxins) remain a major cause of misery and death throughout developing countries, especially in warm climates. A prolonged drought in northern Mexico and the southwestern United States during the early 1990s caused corn to have exceptionally high levels of fuminosin, which can be fatal to horses and pigs, is a probable human carcinogen, and caused infants in these areas to be born with stunted or missing brains, because their mothers had eaten large amounts of infested corn.[24]

Bio-engineered crops can reduce or eliminate these problems, too. Bt corn kills selected insects that chew holes in the corn plants, enabling fungal spores to enter the plant and produce the toxin. It also allows farmers to reduce their use of pesticides by 25 to 50 percent or more. But Greenpeace and other activists have inflamed public opinion against this technology, preying on people's fears that the corn might somehow be toxic to humans or butterflies.

(Ironically, organic food producers routinely spray live Bt over their fields, where breezes can carry the insecticide beyond field boundaries. This "overspray" could conceivably kill non-targeted insects, including butterflies, but in this case the activists have chosen to ignore their vaunted precautionary principle.)

Researchers in India are developing a new biotech peanut that has a built-in vaccine against rinderpest, a disease that kills large numbers of cattle in India and Africa. If they are successful, and if rabid zealots can be persuaded to let farmers plant the new forage crop, millions of people will have much more milk and meat in their diets than ever before.

UNICEF estimates that 30 million infants go without basic immunizations every year. Three million of them die each year from readily preventable diseases, like measles, diphtheria and tetanus. That's more children than die annually from *all* causes in the United States, Europe, Canada and Australia.

Researchers at Iowa State University, Dow Chemical and Monsanto are working to develop new strains of corn and other plants that produce proteins that would cause people's bodies to generate protective antibodies. Someday these antibodies may be capable of staving off intestinal pathogens like the ones that cause severe diarrhea, which kills 2,000,000 to 4,000,000 people a year in developing countries. Other researchers are working on GM plants that could help prevent cystic fibrosis, herpes and hepatitis B.

The advantages of these vaccines are compelling. Children would take them happily, as part of their diet, and not have to suffer the anticipation and pain of an injection. Mothers would not have to trek miles on special trips to clinics. The vaccines would not have to be refrigerated – a valid concern in thousands of villages that lack reliable electricity. Healthcare workers would not have to worry about the too-common practice of reusing needles that are not sterile and thus spread a host of other infectious pathogens like HIV, the virus that causes AIDS, which will leave 20 million African children without one or both parents by 2010. And countries could rely on agricultural delivery systems, which are often better than health care delivery systems, to ensure that the vaccines get to people who need them. The cost of protecting entire populations would plummet. While injected vaccines can cost several dollars a dose – a prohibitive price in destitute nations – biotech researchers believe they could eventually produce vaccines at just pennies a dose, says Charles Arntzen, a professor of plant biology at Arizona State University and director of the Arizona Biodesign Institute in Tempe. Many vaccines could be produced on tiny plats of land. Arntzen estimates he could grow enough hepatitis B vaccine on a mere 25 acres to protect the entire population of China.[25]

However, this progress is also under assault – by Luddite radicals, as well as by fear-mongers in the US and EU food industry and government. All are insisting that stringent new regulations impose new layers of costly, unnecessary, one-size-fits-all requirements on all such "Frankenstein" technologies. If they are successful, the impact on this promising life-saving technology could be incalculable, for benefits too small to be detectable.[26]

Biotechnology could also help save endangered species and protect the wild grasslands, forests and waterways that figure so prominently in environmental literature and fund-raising campaigns, and in the tourism economies of many African countries. "The hunger in southern Africa is driving its desperate inhabitants to hunt down anything that flies, crawls or swims for their stewpots," says Dennis Avery, director of the Center for Global Food Issues.

"The region's normal hunting of 'bushmeat' has escalated now that food is scarcer than AK-47s," he quips in angry frustration. "Thanks to Euro-leadership, Africa is currently projected to clear wildlands greater than the land area of Texas in the next 20 years – for more low-yield, subsistence farming." That would be disastrous for elephants, zebras, lions, wildebeests and scores of other exotic, rare, threatened and endangered African wildlife species.[27]

Economist Indur Goklany has calculated that, if the world tried to feed just today's six billion people using the primarily organic technologies and yields of 1961 (pre-Green Revolution), it would have to cultivate 82 percent of its total land area, instead of the current 38 percent. That would require plowing the Amazon rainforest, irrigating the Sahara Desert and draining Angola's Okavango river basin. The only thing organic farming sustains, says Tuskegee University plant genetics professor and AgBioWorld Foundation president CS Prakash, is "poverty and malnutrition."[28]

None of this is to suggest that biotechnology is a magic bullet that will transform Third World agriculture. It isn't. However, it is a vital weapon in the war against malnutrition, starvation and disease. In conjunction with modern equipment, fertilizers and pesticides, improved transportation infrastructures, integrated crop protection programs, better training in handling chemicals and running farms as businesses, and stronger organizations that give farmers a greater voice in policy decisions – biotechnology and GM crops could play a crucial role in developing countries.

In short, even if the absurd worst-case anti-biotech (or anti-pesticide) scenarios propagated by activists are accepted as valid – and even if a case can somehow be made that these technologies should not be used in the United States or Europe – developing nations should still be permitted to use them. In fact, they should be encouraged to do so. The lives of their people, and their wildlife, hang in the balance.

However, none of these tragic realities seem to have affected the thinking or attitudes of anti-GMO radicals – or of the politicians, bureaucrats and corporate executives who are too timid, preoccupied or unconcerned to challenge the radicals and speak out for more thoughtful policies.

The European Union, in fact, halted approvals of all new bio-engineered foods several years ago. The disruption most likely includes plants with vaccination potential and the ability to expand food production in areas with poor soils, limited rainfall and widespread insect pests. The EU parliament continues to insist on excessive layers of unnecessarily stringent rules for studying, labeling and monitoring genetically altered foods, feeds and pharmaceutical products – and has ignored favorable risk assessments by the EU Scientific Committee.[29]

After the United States and several other countries filed a lawsuit with the World Trade Organization against Europe's biotech ban in May 2003, the EU countered that all it really wants is "adequate" labeling and a system to track genetic modifications from "cradle to grave" – from seed to store shelf. Many companies and scientists support fact-based labeling, to augment existing consumer information. However, the testing, tracing and labeling regime promoted by the EU would be extremely costly and time-consuming, making it financially ruinous for developing countries, while doing nothing to improve food safety. Because all foods would probably have to be certified as "GM-free," the proposal would also send food prices through the roof.

All this seems to suit Friends of the Earth, Environmental Defense, the Sierra Club, the Union of Concerned Scientists and other eco-zealots just fine. In its take-no-prisoners war on biotech crops, Greenpeace says it will stop at nothing less than the "complete elimination" of all biotech products from "the food supply and the environment." Arch Luddite Jeremy Rifkin rants that gene-spliced plants threaten mankind with "a form of annihilation every bit as deadly as nuclear holocaust." Genetic pollution, he says, will create "serious and potentially catastrophic health risks for many of the Earth's animal species and human beings."[30]

The radicals claim their actions promote environmental ethics and corporate social responsibility. But as the comedy team Penn and Teller noted in a television program about GM food, "It's pretty easy to protest when you're not hungry. Naturally, these Greenpeace nuts never let anything as insignificant as the facts get in the way of their party line."[31]

Meanwhile, self-proclaimed anti-biotechnology "expert" Vandana Shiva, a professor of *physics* at a university in India, was honored in August 2002 by *Time* magazine as an "agricultural diversity" and "social justice" "hero." However, the very chemicals and "Green Revolution" plants that she condemns "have allowed Indian farmers to quadruple their production of food grains since independence from Britain, without bringing any more forest land under the plow," says Dr. Prakash.

"Biotechnology now offers the ability to produce more food and better quality food, under demanding conditions and with fewer chemicals," he points out. It is this very technology that Shiva has made a new career in fighting – in the tradition of her namesake, the Hindu god of destruction.

As to Ms. Shiva's expertise, it was highlighted during an October 2000 tour of Rice-Tec biotechnology labs and fields in Texas. "The plants look unhappy," she smugly remarked to the guide and tour group. "The rice plants at home look very happy." The guide replied, "We harvested the rice in August. Those are weeds."[32]

It is these attitudes, this constant emotion and perversion of the truth, that prompted Ismail Serageldin, director of the UN-sponsored Consultative Group on International Agricultural Research, to ask biotech opponents: "Do you want two or three million children a year to go blind and one million to die of vitamin A deficiency, just because you object to the way Golden Rice was created?"[33]

"Want" is probably too strong a word. However, the activists' inflammatory rhetoric, constant fear-mongering and well-orchestrated campaigns against GM foods dramatically underscore their callous indifference to this human suffering and death – and to true social responsibility.

Chapter Four Footnotes

1. Paul Martin and Nicole Itano, "Greens accused of helping Africans starve, *Washington Times,* August 30, 2002. See also James Pinkerton (*Newsday* columnist), "The 'Pure' and the Starving Poor: Environmentalists stifle modern agriculture in the Third World," *Los Angeles Times*, September 3, 2002.

2. "Immoral Europe," *Wall Street Journal* editorial, January 13, 2003; Robert Zoellick, "The human costs of biotech fear-mongering," letter to the editor, *Wall Street Journal*, January 23. 2003.

3. "Seeds of Doubt: As US and EU clash on biotech crops, Africa goes hungry: Tinkering with banana genes could save Uganda staple, but the seeds stay in lab: Using the poor as guinea pigs?" *Wall Street Journal*, December 26, 2002.

4. "Why Africans are starving," editorial, *The Wall Street Journal*, September 17, 2002.

5. See Geoff Hill, "Mugabe's wife outrages countrymen with luxury: Elite accused of south Africa excesses," *Washington Times*, April 29, 2003.

6. "Seeds of Doubt," *Wall Street Journal*, December 26, 2002.

7. See Robert Paarlberg, *The Politics of Precaution: Genetically modified crops in developing countries*, Baltimore, MD: Johns Hopkins University Press (2001).

8. Henry Miller and Gregory Conko, "The UN's bizarre war on biotech," TechCentralStation.com, December 18, 2002.

9. Per Pinstrup-Andersen and Marc Cohen, "Modern Bio-Technology for Food and Agriculture: Risks and opportunities for the poor," in *Agricultural Biotechnology and the Poor*, (Gabrielle Persley and M. Lanti, editors), Washington, DC: Consultative Group on International Agricultural Research and the US National Academy of Sciences, 2000.

10. Patrick Moore, Introduction to Nick Nichols, *Rules for Corporate Warriors: How to fight and survive attack group shakedowns*, Bellevue, WA: Merril Press (2001). See also Patrick Moore, "Battle for Biotech Progress," *IPA Review*, Institute of Public Affairs, Melbourne, Australia, March 2004 (www.ipa.org.au). Moore's www.greenspirit.com website outlines his philosophy.

11. See Thomas DeGregori, *Bountiful Harvest: Technology, food safety and the environment*, Washington, DC: Cato Institute, 2002, pages 107-108 and 114-115.

12. Megan Rosenfeld, "Food Fight: PBS tackles issue of modified food crops," *Washington Post*, April 24, 2001.

13. Lynn Cook, "Millions Served: While the West debates the ethics of genetically modified food, Florence Wambugu is using it to feed her country," *Forbe*s, December 23, 2002.

14. Robert Paarlberg, Department of Political Science Wellesley College, "Statement on Agricultural Biotechnology," presented to the Annual Meeting of The National Governor's Association in Providence, Rhode Island, August 6, 2001.
15. See, *e.g.* Henry Miller and Greg Conko, "Children, Fear and Biotechnology," in *Are Children More Vulnerable to Environmental Chemicals? Scientific and Regulatory Issues in Perspective*, New York: American Council on Science and Health, 2003.
16. Robert Zoellick, "The human costs of biotech fear-mongering," letter to the editor, *Wall Street Journal*, January 23, 2003, citing a December 2002 French report.
17. Florence Wambugu, "Why Africa needs biotech," *Nature*, 400 (6739), 1999.
18. See Henry I. Miller and Gregory Conko, *Biotechnology and the Making of a Public Policy Morass*, New York: Praeger Books (2004 – forthcoming).
19. Robert Zoellick, "United States v. European Union," *Wall Street Journal*, May 21, 2003.
20. Norman Borlaug, speaking in "Eat this!" an April 2003 episode of comedy team Penn and Teller's Showtime original program, "Bullshit!" produced by Star Price, Showtime Networks, Inc.
21. The Rockefeller Foundation, "New rices may help address Vitamin A and Iron Deficiency, major causes of death in the developing world," press release, August 3, 1999.
22. *Ibid.*; Philip Abelson and Pamela Hines, "The Plant Revolution," *Science* (special issue on Plant Biotechnology: Food and Feed), 285 (5156), 1999; Miller and Conko, *op. cit.*, pages 184-185.
23. Golden Rice was developed in the 1990s by Dr. Ingo Potrykus, who gave up his intellectual property rights and persuaded Syngenta and other companies to waive their patents, so that the rice could be made available to poor countries at no cost. The world is still waiting for enviro activists to be so generous and selfless – and for GM opponents to drop their demands for still more evaluations of theoretical risks of Golden Rice.
24. Thomas DeGregori, *Bountiful Harvest*, pages 92, 109, 131; Henry Miller and Greg Conko, "Children, Fear and Biotechnology," pages 186-187. Studies by the United Kingdom's Food Safety Agency in 2003 found that fumonisin levels in organic corn meal were seven to thirty times higher than allowable limits. Levels of this dangerous and carcinogenic mycotoxin in conventionally grown corn, by contrast, were far below allowable limits, and Bt corn is rarely contaminated by fumonisin or other molds. See Alex Avery, "Lessons from the recall," TechCentralStation.com, November 5, 2003; and Dennis Avery,

"Organic farmers cry foul on toxic corn meal recall," Center for Global Food Issues, November 10, 2003 (www.cgfi.org). One can imagine what the reaction of organic farmers and anti-biotech activists would have been, if *GM corn* had so dramatically failed this important food safety test.

25. Rob Wherry, "Planting Hope," *Forbes*, January 3, 2003.

26. See Henry Miller, "Food Fight: We can extract valuable drugs from plants – if fearmongers in the food industry and government don't stop us," *Fortune*, April 14, 2003; Henry Miller, "Will we reap what biopharming sows?" *Nature Biotechnology*, May 2003 (Volume 21, Number 5, pages 480 – 481).

27. Dennis Avery, "Must America fight a trade war with Europe over biotech crops?" Knight-Ridder News Service, October 3, 2002. Avery also points out that Denmark's Bichel Committee found that an organic farming mandate would result in Danish grain production being slashed by 62 percent, pork and poultry production by 70 percent, potato output by 80 percent, because so much of the country's farmland would have to be devoted to grass and hay to feed cattle, so that they would produce more manure to maintain soil fertility. "Danish government report says organic farming is not practical," Center for Global Food Issues, July 16, 2002.

28. Matt Ridley, "We've never had it so good – and it's all thanks to science," *The Guardian* (London), April 3, 2003. For more about biotechnology, see www.agbioworld.org.

29. See Associated Press, "EU Parliament debates food rules," February 13, 2003.

30. See Henry Miller, "Death by Public Policy," Scripps-Howard Newswire, March 14, 2003. To support these anti-biotechnology efforts, the European Union gave radical NGOs $300 million between 1998 and 2002, according to the *Wall Street Journal. See also* Jay Byrne, "Money, Marketing and the Internet: Unanticipated and Unacknowledged Factors Influencing Agricultural Biotechnology Public Acceptance," American Enterprise Institute, June 2003 (from conference on "Biotechnology, the Media and Public Policy").

31. Penn Jillette, "Eat this!" episode of Penn and Teller's Showtime original program, "Bullshit!" (April 2003).

32. Dennis Avery, "Anti-science activists entertain but don't enlighten," Hudson Institute, December 8, 2000.

33. Ron Bailey, "Dr. Strangelunch, or: Why we should learn to stop worrying and love genetically modified food," *Reason*, January 2001.

5

Sustainable Mosquitoes – Expendable People

Fiona "Fifi" Kobusingye is a 34-year-old designer and businesswoman from Kampala, Uganda. In early November 2002, she saw her doctor because she felt fatigued – and discovered she had malaria. Her year-old niece was shivering and crying all night, and suffering from impending kidney failure, because of malaria. Her sister was critically ill and hospitalized with malaria, and her mother came to Kampala to help tend everyone – but ended up in the hospital herself with malaria.

"Our family and community are suffering and dying from this disease, and too many Europeans and environmentalists only talk about protecting the environment," Kobusingye says. "But what about the people? The mosquitoes are everywhere. You think you're safe, and you're not. Europeans and Americans can afford to deceive themselves about malaria and pesticides. But we can't."[1]

Compared to many others, though, her family is lucky – so far. It can afford medical treatment, and everyone is feeling better, for now at least. But other families aren't so fortunate.

In 2000, say World Health Organization and other studies, malaria infected over 300 million people. It killed nearly 2,000,000 – most of them in sub-Saharan Africa. Over half of the victims are children, who die at the rate of two per minute or 3,000 per day – the equivalent of 80 fully loaded school buses plunging over a cliff every day of the year. Since 1972, over 50 million people have died from this dreaded disease. Many are weakened by AIDS or dysentery, but actually die of malaria.[2]

In addition to these needless deaths, malaria also saps economies and health care resources. It keeps millions home from work and school every day. Chronic anemia can sap people's strength for years and leave victims with severe liver and kidney damage, while cerebral malaria can cause lifelong learning and memory problems, follwed by early death.

The disease drains the Indian economy of as much as $737 million every year, in lost wages due to deaths and absence from work, reduced productivity due to fatigue, and money spent on insecticides, medicines and malaria research, New Delhi's Liberty Institute has calculated.[3]

Africa's gross national product would be $400 billion a year – instead of its current $300 billion annually – if malaria had been wiped out in 1965, when it was eliminated in most of the developed world. Malaria control costs Africa $12 billion annually, depleting budgets for other health, environmental, economic and social programs. It particularly afflicts poor families, who must use up to 25 percent or more of their income on prevention and treatment.[4]

Uganda alone spends nearly $350 million a year on malaria, and devotes up to 40 percent of its outpatient care to malaria patients. In 2002, 80,000 Ugandans died of the disease, and again half of them were children.[5] "Most families can't even afford to get proper treatment. Where do you get the money to go back to the hospital again and again," asks Kobusingye, "when your family needs food and so many other things?"

These are real deaths and real impacts – not just theoretical deaths, based on extrapolations from rodent studies (as in the case of Alar, the growth-regulating chemical that was the subject of a vitriolic attack and fund-raising campaign by the Natural Resources Defense Council and Fenton Communications in 1989[6]), or hypothetical catastrophes (like flood and drought scenarios generated by certain climate change computer models).

They are due in large part to near-global restrictions on the production, export and use of DDT. Originally imposed in the United States by EPA Administrator William Ruckelshaus in 1972,[7] the DDT prohibitions have been expanded and enforced by NGO pressure, coercive treaties, and threats of economic sanctions by foundations, nations and international aid agencies.

Where DDT is used, malaria deaths plummet. Where it is not used, they skyrocket. For example, in South Africa, the most developed nation on the continent, the incidence of malaria had been kept very low (below 10,000 cases annually) by the careful use of DDT. But in 1996 environmentalist pressure convinced program directors to cease using DDT. One of the worst epidemics in the country's history ensued, with almost 62,000 cases in 2000.

Shortly after this peak, South Africa reintroduced DDT. In one year, malaria cases plummeted 80 percent; with the introduction of Artemesinin-based Combination Therapy drugs, in three years they were down by 93 percent! Next door, in Mozambique, which uses pyrethroids but not DDT, malaria rates remain high. Similar experiences have been recorded in Zambia, other African countries, Sri Lanka, Bangladesh and elsewhere.[8]

DDT likewise helped to eradicate malaria from vast areas of South America, though not in Central America, and to control the disease in additional areas via indoor spraying. Control continued as long as the centralized spray programs were maintained. However, as environmental groups and the World Health Organization succeeded in eliminating both outdoor and indoor uses of DDT, the number of malaria cases spiraled upward. Manaus, Brazil, and many other areas are now enduring the return of endemic malaria to pre-DDT levels.

"The re-emergence of this devastating disease," says Donald Roberts, Professor of Tropical Public Health at the Uniformed Services University of Health Sciences, "is clear and unambiguous testimony to the falsehoods of environmentalists and the failed policies of the WHO."

No other chemical comes close to DDT as an affordable, effective way to *repel* mosquitoes from homes, *exterminate* any that land on walls, and *disorient* any that are not killed or repelled, largely eliminating their urge to bite in homes that are treated once or twice a year with tiny amounts of this miracle insecticide. For impoverished countries, many of which are struggling to rebuild economies wracked by decades of disease and civil war, cost and effectiveness are critical considerations.

Substitute pesticides help but are problemmatical. While carbamates work well, they are four to six times more expensive than DDT and must be sprayed much more often. Organophosphates are dangerous and thus not appropriate in homes. And mosquitoes have built up a huge resistance to synthetic pyrethroids, because they are used so extensively in agriculture.

For poor African, Asian and Latin American countries, cost alone can be determinative. Not only do they need their limited funds for other public health priorities, like safe drinking water, but they have minimal health and medical infrastructures. Every dollar spent trying to control malaria is a dollar that's unavailable for other public health needs. "DDT is long-acting; the alternatives are not," says Professor Roberts. "DDT is cheap; the alternatives are not. End of story."[9]

DDT is not a panacea, or a "super weapon" that can replace all others. Nor is it suitable in all situations. However, it is a vital weapon – often the "best available technology" – in a war that must be fought against a number of mosquito species (vectors) and constantly changing malaria parasites, in different terrains and cultures, and under a wide variety of housing and other conditions. Like any army, healthcare workers need to have access to every available weapon. To saddle them with one-size-fits-all solutions (tanks and pistols, bed nets and drug therapies) is unconscionable.

The chemical is no longer used in agriculture (which accounted for 99 percent of its use at the time Rachel Carson wrote *Silent Spring*). Today it is used almost entirely, and very selectively, in malaria control, via spraying in tiny quantities on the insides of the traditional huts and houses that are common in areas of Africa most threatened by the disease.

It is not carcinogenic or harmful to humans; used in accord with these modern practices, it is safe for the environment; and malaria-carrying mosquitoes are far less likely to build immunities to DDT than to other pesticides that environmentalists and US, EU and UN agencies tolerate only as a last resort. Rare cases of immunity in decades past have since been linked to gross overuse in agriculture during the 1950s and 1960s. DDT's alleged toxicity to wildlife may have been due to faulty lab studies, its being mixed with dangerous petroleum distillates, or rampant discharges of other chemicals into waterways. "In the 60 years since DDT was first introduced," notes South African Richard Tren, president of Africa Fighting Malaria, "not a single scientific paper has been able to replicate even one case of actual human harm from its use."[10]

During World War II, DDT was actually classified as a secret weapon, because of its unparalleled ability to prevent malaria and typhus among Allied troops. After the war, virtually every concentration camp survivor and many other Europeans were also doused multiple times with DDT to prevent typhus, with no ill effects reported. The widespread use of DDT in Europe and the United States played vital roles in eradicating malaria and typhus on both continents.

In 1979, a World Health Organization (WHO) review of DDT use failed to find "any possible adverse effects of DDT" and deemed it to be the "safest pesticide used for residual spraying in vector control programs." Estimates by reputable scientists and scientific organizations have gone as high as five hundred million lives saved by the use of DDT.[11]

Nevertheless, the WHO, United Nations Environmental Program (UNEP), World Bank, Greenpeace, Pesticide Action Network, World Wildlife Fund, Physicians for Social Responsibility and other groups remain adamantly opposed to the use of DDT – and other pesticides. Their stance angers many who must live with malaria's consequences every day. However, these organizations ignore the victims' growing anger and the rising body count. Instead, they continue to advocate steps that, while helpful, simply cannot be the sole solution to this widespread and complex disease.

• Insecticide-treated mosquito bed nets do help at night, if used properly and regularly. But they are not foolproof or repellant, must be re-treated regularly, and are hardly appropriate during the day, at work, in school or at play.
• Drug therapies are extremely expensive for poor families and poor countries. They also depend on public health facilities that are lacking in most malarial regions, and on committed patients and parents treating themselves and their children on a regular basis. Moreover, the parasite that causes malaria has become increasingly resistant to chloroquine and other drugs, the cheapest and most common medical treatments.
• Fish that eat mosquito larvae at best offer a haphazard approach that helps under certain, limited circumstances.

But the government and donor agencies and environmental activists still do not support the use of pesticides, and certainly not DDT. Indeed, they are trying to phase out all pesticides, via international treaties and other means.

A principal argument against DDT is that its use is not "sustainable." This claim has frequently been made by Gro Harlem Brundtland, who was instrumental in promoting the sustainable development concept when she was Norway's prime minister – and headed the World Health Organization between 1998 and 2003. However, without DDT, the lives of millions in developing countries are certainly not sustainable.

"My friend's four-year-old child hasn't been able to walk for months, because of malaria," Fifi Kobusingye says softly, her voice breaking. "She crawls around on the floor. Her eyes bulge out like a chameleon, her hair is dried up, and her stomach is all swollen because the parasites have taken over her liver. Her family doesn't have the money to help her, and neither does the Ugandan government. All they can do is take care of her the best they can, and wait for her to die."[12]

Professor Roberts has heard many stories like this, and seen similar tragedies unfold right before his eyes. He is outraged at the "high pressure tactics" that have forced many countries to abandon public-health uses of DDT – and watch their disease and death tolls soar. He is not alone.

"If we don't use DDT, the results will be measured in loss of life," David Nabarro, director of Roll Back Malaria, says bluntly. "The cost of the alternatives tend to run six times that of DDT."[13] That fact, however, appears to be irrelevant to many activist groups and aid agencies.

Activists like actor Ed Begley, Jr. and the Pesticide Action Network like to say there is no global ban on DDT. But they are playing semantic games. Increasing restrictions on the production, storage, transportation and use of DDT and other pesticides, lengthy delays in getting approvals to use them, mounds of costly red tape, and the refusal of donor agencies and foundations to fund indoor residual spraying programs all add up to one thing: sickness and death for millions of Africans every year. From the activists' perspective, says Richard Tren, that's just "bad luck for the people who have to die, so that über bureaucrats in Geneva can dot their i's and cross their t's."

"The US Agency for International Development will not fund any indoor residual spraying and neither will most of the other donors," Tren notes. "This means that most African countries have to use whatever [these donors] are willing to fund (bed nets), which may not be the most appropriate tool." Belize and Bolivia have both admitted that they stopped using DDT in the face of USAID pressure, and many other developing countries refrain from using DDT because "they don't want to damage their chances of exporting agricultural produce to the North." Mozambique beats around the bush, in giving absurd reasons why it won't use DDT, even as tens of thousands of its citizens are dying.[14]

USAID director Andrew Natsios' pointed comments about GM corn and starvation thus stand in sharp contrast to the agency's position on the use of DDT to combat malaria. The agency refuses to fund DDT programs, because the WHO does not support its use, and the insecticide is not permitted in the United States, where malaria and West Nile virus problems pale in comparison to mosquito-borne diseases in developing countries. Its current stance also contrasts sharply with its previous support for DDT and other chemicals between 1950 and 1972, when it contributed $1.2 billion to the Global Malaria Eradication Campaign. German, Swedish, Norwegian and other aid agencies take a similar position.[15]

All these donor agencies, suggests Tren, "need to decide whether they are in Africa to save lives, or to be politically correct and please the Greens at home."[16]

What is permitted today in risk-averse countries that have already conquered malaria should simply be irrelevant for nations that are suffering massive epidemics today. As Tren and Roger Bate ask, would Sweden really refuse to fund hospital nurses in Africa if they worked under conditions that do not fulfill Swedish health and safety requirements?[17] Would donor agencies refuse to fund immunization programs, because some people have allergic reactions to vaccines?

India's Department of Trade and Industry worries that the country's agricultural produce will be turned away from Europe if any traces of DDT are found, Tren notes. And in a truly bizarre example of misplaced priorities and concerns, Zimbabwe's department of health was told to stop using DDT because growers were worried that their *carcinogenic* tobacco would get rejected by the USA and EU if any DDT were found on it.[18]

Domestic US laws also prevent the import of produce with residues of pesticides and other chemicals that have been banned in the United States. This has forced growers to spray more often with non-persistent pesticides that are more expensive and more toxic to workers, resulting in more cases of pesticide poisonings, especially in poor countries where hand spraying is the norm. Whether it will also result in bans on the import of fish and agricultural products from South Africa, Uganda and other countries that dare to use DDT is an open question.[19]

Ugandan Health Minister Jim Muhwezi summed the matter up succinctly, when he announced in late 2002 that his country would begin using DDT to control mosquitoes. Uganda did so despite warnings by environmentalists and the European Union that it risks having a boycott launched against its coffee and having its fish and agricultural exports banned in EU and other foreign markets, if it goes forward with its plan. Kenya is also considering the use of DDT to combat its growing epidemic; that would make it only the eighth African nation to do so.

In Muhwezi's view, the cost of treating malaria, and the burden it places on the country, outweigh any environmental repercussions, which indeed are almost nil. He cited the successful use of DDT in Mauritius and South Africa to slash malaria disease and death rates and said, "Our people's lives are of primary importance. The West is concerned about the environment because we share it with them. But it is not concerned about malaria because it is not a problem there. In Europe, they used DDT to kill anopheles mosquitoes that cause malaria. Why can't we use DDT to kill the enemy in our camp?"[20]

The United States and Europe successfully used DDT to eradicate malaria. For them to downplay the lethal effects of this disease on developing nations – while obsessing about theoretical health problems from trace chemicals in food and drinking water – strikes Tren, Muhwezi and others as hypocritical, paternalistic and callous. It is hardly ethical or socially responsible.

New insecticides, chemicals and drugs are clearly needed. However their development and use are hampered by insufficient funding (in Africa), excessive reliance on the precautionary principle (particularly in Europe), and drug approval delays and the ever-present threat of multi-billion-dollar liability judgments (especially in the United States). Even if they might someday be a reliable substitute for DDT, tens of millions are likely to die in the meantime.

Simply put, the suggestion that alternatives to DDT exist now or are "just around the corner" is little more than wishful thinking in its deadliest form – promoted by people who have staked out an ideological position against DDT anywhere, anytime and under any circumstances, and cling to their position like limpets to a rock.

As author, film producer and PhD molecular biologist Michael Crichton put it: "Banning DDT is one of the most disgraceful episodes in the twentieth century history of America. We knew better, and we did it anyway, and we let people around the world die, and we didn't give a damn."[21]

Even the *New York Times* (which usually sides with radical environmental groups) now says the developed world "has been unconscionably stingy in financing the fight against malaria or research into alternatives to DDT. Until one is found, wealthy nations should be helping poor countries with all available means – including DDT."[22]

And still anti-pesticide activists like Greenpeace and the World Wildlife Fund are unmoved.

Many Africans, Asians and Latin Americans are understandably outraged. They view the intense pressure on countries not to use DDT as a lethal form of eco-imperialism, imposed by nations that eradicated malaria, dengue fever and typhus decades ago – against nations that continue to be devastated by these deadly diseases. The restrictions on pesticides are also a grotesque abuse of the precautionary principle, akin to telling terminally ill cancer patients they may not use morphine to ease their pain, because *you* are concerned about the use of addictive drugs by well-to-do high school students.

The United States death toll from West Nile virus (260 people in 2001 and 2002 combined) is a mere 0.007 percent of Africa's annual death toll from malaria. And yet, Americans are again using pesticide spraying programs to control mosquitoes that spread the virus. They would never tolerate being told they had to protect their children solely by using bed nets, larvae-eating fish and medicinal treatments. But they have been silent about conditions in Africa, and about the intolerable attitudes of environmental groups, aid agencies and their own government.

"Corporate social responsibility ought not be used to impose policies that kill people," says Kenya's James Shikwati. "It should not be used to render poor populations sick, unproductive and perpetually destitute. For rich countries to tell poor nations to ... ban chemicals that help control disease-carrying insects – and then claim to be responsible, humanitarian and compassionate – is to engage in hypocrisy of the most lethal kind."[23]

Niger Innis, national spokesman for the Congress of Racial Equality, is equally blunt. "There is no more basic human right," he emphasizes, "than to live – to not be murdered by design, indifference or callous disregard. And yet, [civil rights leaders] and Amnesty International are missing in action. So are the CEOs of BP, Shell Oil, Ford Motors and other members of the World Business Council for Sustainable Development.

"Surely, sustaining, improving and saving lives is the most fundamental form of corporate social responsibility," Innis continues. "Why have they not challenged the radicals who set the Council's agenda and promote these lethal policies? Aren't they just a little uncomfortable being complacent accessories to what many Africans view as eco-manslaughter?"[24]

The anti-pesticide activists and donor groups know full well the consequences of their actions – just as a driver knows full well what is likely to happen if he takes his car at full throttle the wrong way down a busy street. But still the radicals persist in their deadly "game" with people's lives.

And yet, for their intense opposition to DDT use – and despite their blatant lack of concern for people – companies, politicos, NGOs, Hollywood celebrities, foundations and government bureaucrats are frequently hailed as "socially responsible," concerned about people's health and well-being, and "passionate about the environment."

It would be laughable, if it weren't so tragic.

Chapter Five Footnotes

1. Fifi Kobusingye, personal interview with Paul Driessen, May 6, 2003.
2. See www.FightingMalaria.org and extensive studies and articles cited and linked by that website, including "Malaria and the DDT Story," by Dr. Kelvin Kemm of Stratek Technology Strategy Consultants, in *Environment Health* (Lorraine Mooney and Roger Bate, editors). See also Walter Williams, "Killing people," *The Washington Times*, October 17, 2002; Deroy Murdock, "Nutritional Schizophrenia," NationalReviewOnline, June 25, 2002.
3. Barun Mitra and Richard Tren, *The Burden of Malaria*, Delhi, India: Liberty Institute, Occasional Paper 12, November 2002.
4. John Gallup and Jeffrey Sachs, *The Economic Burden of* Malaria, Harvard University Center for International Development, London School for Hygiene and Tropical Medicine, for the World Health Organization, 2000. For a detailed examination of the health, social and economic impacts of malaria – especially on African countries – see Richard Tren and Roger Bate, *When Politics Kills: Malaria and the DDT story*, Sandton, South Africa: Africa Fighting Malaria (2000). A more recent version of *Malaria and the DDT story* can be downloaded from the Institute of Economic Affairs website at http://www.iea.org.uk/record.php?type=publication&ID=11
5. Alexander Gourevitch, "Should the DDT ban be lifted?" *Washington Monthly*, April 9, 2003.
6. The chemical Alar was used to regulate the growth and ripening of apples, until it became the subject of an attack launched by Fenton Communications, the NRDC and CBS's "60 Minutes." In a later interview, David Fenton admitted that "the PR campaign was designed so that revenue would flow back to NRDC from the public." See Bonner Cohen, John Carlisle, *et al.*, *The Fear Profiteers: Do "socially responsible" businesses sow health scares to reap monetary rewards?* Arlington, VA: Lexington Institute (2000).
7. In so doing, Ruckelshaus ignored thousands of pages of scientific evidence attesting to the pesticide's safety, as well as expert recommendations that its use be continued for malaria control.
8. Richard Tren, president, Africa Fighting Malaria, personal communication, December 20, 2002; Brian Sharp, P. van Wyk, et al., "Malaria control by residual insecticide spraying in Chingola and Chililabombwe, Copperbelt Province, Zambia," *Journal of Tropical Medicine and International Health*, pages 732-736, September 2002. Richard Tren and Roger Bate, "Relief South Africans found for malaria is spelled DDT," *Investors Busniness Daily*, March 25, 2004. Indoor residual spraying programs pose virtually no environmental risks.

9. Alexander Gourevitch, "Should the DDT ban be lifted?" and Donald Roberts, personal communication to Paul Driessen, April 29, 2003.
10. Richard Tren, "DDT still saving lives," a UPI Outside View commentary, November 11, 2002. See also Bjorn Lomborg, *The Skeptical Environmentalist: Measuring the real state of the world*, Cambridge, UK: Cambridge University Press (2001), pages 233-235, 237, 243-244.
11. See Thomas R. DeGregori, *Bountiful Harvest: Technology, food safety and the environment*, Washington, DC: Cato Institute, 2002, page 132.
12. Fifi Kobusingye, interview with Paul Driessen, May 6, 2003.
13. David Nabarro, director, Roll Back Malaria; quoted in "Malaria Meeting: Africans Discuss a Disease Biting Into Lives and Economies," ABCNews.com, April 2000.
14. Richard Tren, personal communication, December 17, 2002; Roger Bate, "Without DDT, malaria bites back," www.spiked-online.com, April 24, 2001.
15. Richard Tren and Roger Bate, *When Politics Kills: Malaria and the DDT story*, page 24. All other countries combined contributed only $2.8 million, via the World Health Organization, they note.
16. Personal email to Paul Driessen, April 7, 2003.
17. Richard Tren and Roger Bate, *Malaria and the DDT Story*, London: Institute of Economic Affairs, 2001, page 58.
18. Richard Tren, president, Africa Fighting Malaria, personal communication, December 17, 2002.
19. DeGregori, page 147, citing Matt Crenson, "Thousands of Children Jeopardized by Pesticide Use," Associated Press, Nando.net online, December 18, 1997. Amazingly, the 1996 Food Quality Protection Act specifically forbids the USEPA from considering occupational exposures to pesticides on the part of the children and adults who grow and pick the produce Americans eat.
20. David Kaiza, "Uganda to use DDT despite ban," *The East African*, Nairobi, Kenya, December 2, 2002; Tom Carter, "Kenyan research center favors DDT use: Malaria toll trumps ecological threat," *Washington Times*, May 9, 2003.
21. Michael Crichton, "Our Greatest Challenge," Remarks to the Commonwealth Club of San Francisco, September 15, 2003.
22. *New York Times* editorial, December 23, 2002. *See also* Tina Rosenberg, "What the world needs now is DDT," *New York Times Magazine*, April 10, 2004, chronicling the virtues of this repellant-pesticide.
23. James Shikwati, "How Europe is killing Africans," *The Day* (New London, CT), February 3, 2003.
24. Niger Innis, "Jesse and Al: Missing in action," Congress of Racial Equality commentary, July 2003.

6

Sweat Shops and Prostitutes

Corporate social responsibility tenets demand that "uniform rules" apply across international borders for the transport of industrial materials and for wages paid by multinational companies (MNCs) in their domestic and overseas factories. Rarely is any consideration given to the perverse consequences that these policies have on ordinary people in developing nations.

The notion of "uniform rules" and a "level playing field," in reality, is often little more than a club wielded by anti-trade radicals. It can also be a clever subterfuge by developed countries to protect their own industries by imposing hidden tariffs on imported goods, under the guise of safeguarding environmental quality, workers' health and human rights, preventing "sweatshop" conditions in overseas plants, or demanding "living wages." The result is the elimination of economic opportunities for the Third World's poor, and the loss of developing countries' single most important competitive advantage: their low cost labor.[1]

The imposition of US or EU standards thus harms those whom the self-proclaimed champions of the world's poor purport to represent. It may well be that wages and working conditions in foreign countries are far below what anyone in the developed world would like to see, far below what would be tolerated in America or Europe. However, they are frequently better than conditions that previously existed in their countries.

So-called sweatshop wages are also better than the alternatives: no jobs, worse jobs, malnutrition, thievery and, for many women and young girls, prostitution (if that's what it takes to put food on the family table).

> • Public debate over a proposed US "Child Labor Deterrence Act" triggered pressure on multinational corporations, prompting a German garment maker to lay off 50,000 child workers in Bangladesh. Oxfam International later found that thousands of these children became prostitutes, turned to crime or starved to death.
> • According to UNICEF, an international boycott of Nepalese carpets in the mid-1990s caused plants to shut down, driving thousands of young girls into the sex trade.
> • In 1995, anti-sweatshop groups on college campuses helped pressure Nike, Reebok and other companies to close their plants in Pakistan. Tens of thousands of Pakistanis lost their jobs and average family incomes in the country fell by 20 percent. Again, thousands ended up as thieves, beggars or prostitutes.[2]
> • Today, in Hunnan and other parts of China, young children are forced to leave school, and end up working in fields, local industries or worse, because their parents are sick, disabled, laid off or dead, and their small contribution is the only thing standing between survival and malnutrition for their impoverished families.

"Socially responsible" investors often chant the mantra, "doing well by doing good." The sad reality, however, is that they frequently cause grievous harm by arrogantly presuming to do good. Their ideology interferes with their analytical skills and ability to discern the likely consequences of their policies.

Corporations get fined and executives may do jail time for careless oversights that result in human or environmental harm. But college and SRI pressure groups rarely have to worry about errors, oversights and accountability. Nor do regulators, journalists, judges, professors and politicians who support the activists.

In many cases, "sweatshop" wages are actually higher than what most people in these countries can hope to earn elsewhere. What Nike was paying its Indonesian workers in 2000 was more than double the daily income of half of that nation's working population. In Vietnam, Nike paid an average monthly salary of $65 – twice the monthly salary of a teacher and more than doctors in state-run hospitals were receiving. In Honduras, its starting factory wages were well above the average per capita income of $600, making these jobs a golden opportunity for people who had no chance to land a job flipping burgers for the Golden Arches in the States.[3]

Simply put, however small these salaries might be compared to those in the US or EU, they greatly increase workers' standards of living in countries where the cost of living is well below that in developed nations. They also enable families to raise their incomes high enough that, within a generation or two, children can go to school instead of having to work. Indeed, virtually every developed country, from Britain and Sweden to the United States and Taiwan, went through a sweatshop period on their way to becoming modern, educated, industrialized and prosperous.

The "machinations of special-interest groups" may work well to protect domestic job security, says Stephan Spath, executive director of the Foundation for Economic Education. But they also "prevent workers in developing countries from finding better opportunities to raise their living standards." If MNCs are forced to pay US wages in countries where job skills, productivity, education levels, and local economic and labor-market conditions cannot justify such wages, Spath continues, "there would be no production cost savings and hence no purpose in relocating to those countries in the first place."

Their poverty-stricken people would then lose the jobs and other benefits of direct foreign investment, including improved local economic conditions, a chance to develop their technical skills, and better roads, schools, hospitals, sanitary facilities, and disease control and treatment programs near the new factories (many of them established by the MNCs).[4]

CSR and the precautionary principle also have perverse unintended consequences in the area of waste recycling. The low value of labor in developing nations justifies the long hours spent extracting material and recycling metals and chemicals. "Free trade in waste would allow the comparative advantage of societies to make waste processing economically viable and efficient," notes Barun Mitra of New Delhi's Liberty Institute. It would allow poor societies to take advantage of opportunities to create new industries, and build new economic foundations for their people. However, recently enacted treaties and rules "thwart this process."[5]

The Basel Convention on the Transboundary Movement of Hazardous Wastes prompted European companies to stop exporting chemicals, lead and zinc – and India to stop importing them. India's low consumption of automotive batteries and other products has thus meant that its own industrial and consumer markets are no longer able to support recycling plants in the absence of imported raw materials. Plants have closed, jobs have disappeared, and India's ability to remove chemical and metallic contaminants from its own environment, and the world's, has been drastically curtailed.

Activist demands for "comparable" wages and working conditions are now threatening another major Indian industry: the dismantling of huge ocean-going vessels to recycle their steel and other metals. "Trade creates wealth, and if free trade, including trade in waste, is allowed ... greater productivity and more advanced technology will ensure [greater recycling rates,] reasonably priced disposal of waste that cannot be traded," and better standards of living for millions of people in Third World nations.[6]

As China native and University of Hawaii professor Kate Zhou notes, trade helps the poor. "It is anti-poor and racist to impose boycotts and lofty western standards on families and communities that are trying to build better lives for their children and grandchildren. If radicals get their way, poor people will suffer most."

Adds Shalini Wadhwa, human rights advocate and managing editor of a Nepalese magazine for entrepreneurs: "Trade is an inherent instinct, even for children. In countries like Nepal, Iraq, China, India and Nigeria, it is the poorest people who trade the most, usually through small, family-owned businesses. They survive on trade. Take away freedom to trade, freedom to earn a living by whatever means, and you take away their ability to survive."[7]

"Rather than improving African economies, foreign aid only worsens their situation," argues Kenya's James Shikwati. After decades on the dole, "70 countries are poorer than they were in 1980, and 43 are worse off than they were in 1970. The anti-globalization crusaders could help Africa more if they would advocate for the promotion of free trade and abolition of subsidies in the West. Lift the protective barrier in the developed countries and allow consumers to sample African products. To empower the poor economically, give them a chance to trade," he pleads.[8]

Restrictions on free trade mean that fundamental human rights are glossed over or ignored. Those basic freedoms include the right to jobs, adequate food, and better health and economic conditions. They also include the right of sovereign nations and communities to set priorities without being second-guessed or dictated to by bureaucrats and NGOs from developed countries.

All thoughtful people want sustained economic growth and improved health and environmental quality. The three are inextricably linked, as the annual "Index of Economic Freedom" consistently demonstrates. Of 161 countries studied in 2002, the ones that prospered most were those that assured the most economic freedom and opportunity for their people. Among the success stories are Hong Kong, Ireland, Luxembourg, New Zealand, Singapore and the United States – with Estonia, Mexico and Russia making notable gains. Among the laggards (not surprisingly) were Argentina, Brazil, Cuba, Venezuela and most African nations.[9]

Wealth creates health and environmental quality. And achieving sustained prosperity requires limited taxes and regulations, a predictable legal and judicial system without corruption or abuse of power, enforceable contracts, a stable currency, relative ease in setting up new businesses, and the right of sovereign nations and communities to make their own decisions. Many of these fundamental requirements are sadly lacking in poor developing nations and their constitutions.

Perhaps most of all, however, a better future for these nations depends on their having secure property rights and unraveling what Peruvian economist Hernando de Soto calls *The Mystery of Capital*. What is it, de Soto asks, that prevents capitalism from delivering to developing countries the same wealth it has delivered to the West? "Why does capitalism thrive only in the West, as if enclosed in a bell jar?"

Capital, he argues, "is the force that raises the productivity of labor and creates the wealth of nations. It is the lifeblood of the capitalist system, the foundation of progress, and the one thing that the poor countries of the world cannot seem to produce for themselves." This is so despite the fact that, in Asia, Africa, the Middle East and Latin America alike, millions of poor people already possess the assets they need to make a success of capitalism.

In fact, they own "forty times all the foreign aid received throughout the world since 1945," he notes. Unfortunately, they own these resources in "defective forms: houses built on lands whose ownership rights are not adequately recorded, unincorporated businesses with undefined liability, industries located where financiers and investors cannot see them." These poor would-be entrepreneurs have "dead capital" – "houses but not titles; crops but not deeds; businesses but not statutes of incorporation."

Because the ownership rights to these possessions and resources are not documented adequately or officially, the assets "cannot readily be turned into capital, cannot be traded outside of narrow local circles where people know and trust each other, cannot be used as collateral for a loan, and cannot be used as a share against investment."

This, says de Soto, is the "mystery of capital." In simple terms, it is private property rights, decentralized legal ownership of private property and natural resources, and a legal right to form a corporation. Instead of remaining hooked on the opium of foreign aid, these countries need to reform their legal, economic and property rights systems.

Adam Smith and other Westerners were able to "comprehend and gain access to those things we know exist but cannot see," by representing assets with titles – and thereby "seeing" them, assigning value to them, and converting that value into capital, to finance other endeavors. It was this discovery that led to what American historian Gordon Wood described as "something momentous" in society and culture – a new legal and economic system that released "the aspirations and energies of common people as never before." Concludes de Soto, "This was the moment when the West crossed the demarcation line that led to successful capitalism."[10]

Will developing countries now cross that same demarcation line and achieve this same momentous opportunity? Or will activists and other dictators continue to deny western success to the rest of the world? Will they, indeed, deny future success and progress to western nations? Two documents underscore the dangers facing a better future. Both reject capitalism, free trade, globalization, multinational corporations, property rights and other generators of a better future for people the world over.

The first is a 300-page manifesto known as *Agenda 21.* Propelled by alarmist calls to "save the planet" from environmental "devastation," it proposes that national governments pursue "sustainability" by controlling land and energy use, economic production and consumption, and people's daily lives. It would do so through centralized government plans and edicts, monitored and enforced through the United Nations and global non-governmental organizations.[11]

The second, related document is a paper delivered in March 2002 by Randall Hayes, president of the radical Rainforest Action Network, at the Johns Hopkins Symposium on Foreign Affairs. *Restructuring the Global Economy: Eradicating Breton Woods and Creating New Institutions* is a detailed roadmap to a Green future, as envisioned by Hayes and Jerry Mander, founder of the International Forum on Globalization, a coalition of some 60 anti-capitalist organizations and intellectuals from 25 nations.[12]

"Capitalism is the ruling system," they lecture, and "economic globalization is the greatest single contributor to the massive ecological crises of our time." In their view, the source of the problem is the "Breton Woods" institutions: the World Bank, International Monetary Fund (IMF) and General Agreement on Tariffs and Trade (GATT), out of which came the WTO or World Trade Organization.

Their solution is to "wrest control of global economic rule making away from" these organizations and "transnational corporate executive powerbrokers" – dismantle most of the Breton Woods institutions – and transfer power to a "strengthened" United Nations, World Health Organization, International Labor Organization, Food and Agriculture Organization, United Nations Development Program, United Nations Environment Program and other global organizations. This is necessary, they assert, because they now "realize that the most important environmental policy is, in fact, economic policy." Their goal is to "radically improve, humanize and ecologize" capitalism; become the powerbrokers for future economic and environmental policy; and partake increasingly in the taxpayer-funded projects and grants provided by these governmental institutions.

Few would argue that the World Bank, IMF or WTO are perfect institutions. But for anyone who observed how the United Nations handled Rwanda, Bosnia, Iraq or the Sudan – or has followed its statements and actions on pesticides, malaria, global warming and the HIV/AIDS crisis – the Mander/Hayes vision is chilling. If these activists get their way, destitute people the world over will face a future marked by an absence of freedom and opportunity, and by perpetual deprivation and despair.

"Africa needs the liberty that the US enjoys," South Africa's Richard Tren noted in an editorial commenting on a May 2003 protest against Greenpeace by the Congress of Racial Equality. "We need the liberty and freedom to use whatever [energy, pesticide or food] technology we require, without interference and restrictions from organizations like Greenpeace that have little interest in human life. We need free trade and individual liberties that made the US the wealthiest and most powerful nation on earth. We don't need the racist, misguided and life-threatening anti-growth campaigns run by eco-imperialist Greenpeace."[13]

And yet, in the view of many politicians, journalists and Hollywood elites, the Mander Hayes & Company vision marks the culmination of a world governed under the doctrines of corporate social responsibility, sustainable development, the precautionary principle and socially responsible investing.

Chapter Six Footnotes

1. See David Henderson, *Misguided Virtue: False notions of corporate responsibility,* London: Institute of Economic Affairs (2001), pages 111-116.
2. Radley Balko, "The Road from Serfdom," TechCentralStation.com, April 29, 2003; Johann Norberg, *In Defence of Global Capitalism,* Stockholm, Sweden: Timbro (2001), pages 186-189.
3. Matt Geyer, "Sweatshop protests unwarranted," *The Austin Review* (online), April 1, 2000.
4. Stephan Spath, "The Virtues of Sweatshops," *Ideas on Liberty,* Foundation for Economic Education, March 2002.
5. Barun Mitra (Liberty Institute, Delhi, India), "Poverty, Wealth and Waste," *PERC Reports,* March 2000.
6. *Ibid.* For an African perspective on economic development issues, see www.irenkenya.org, the website of James Shikwati and the Inter Region Economic Network of Kenya.
7. Kate Zhou and Shalini Wadhwa, speaking at the Atlas Economic Research Foundation's Third Annual Liberty Forum, "Communicating the Benefits of Free Trade," New Orleans, LA, April 23-24, 2003.
8. James Shikwati, "Subsidizing poverty in Africa," Inter Region Economic Network, Nairobi, Kenya, July 2, 2002.
9. Gerald O'Driscoll and Edwin Feulner (Heritage Foundation), Mary Anastasia O'Grady and Robert Bartley (*Wall Street Journal*), *Index of Economic Freedom,* Washington, DC: Heritage Foundation (2003).
10. Hernando de Soto, *The Mystery of Capital: Why capitalism triumphs in the West and fails everywhere else,* New York: Basic Books (2000), pages 5-10. See also Arnold Kling, "What Causes Prosperity?" and "Government *Is* the Solution," www.TechCentralStation.com, April 2003.
11. For an analysis of the Hayes paper, see http://undueinfluence.com/global_green_goals.htm; for the complete paper see ranamuck.org/restructuring.htm; see also Alan Oxley, "WTO = WEO?" TechCentralStation.com, April 9, 2003.
12. For the complete text of *Agenda 21* and related documents, see www.sovereignty.net/p/SD. IFOG is funded by the MacArthur Foundation, Rockefeller Brothers Fund, Ford Foundation, and other foundations whose great wealth, ironically, comes from the very capitalist institutions Hayes and Mander so detest.
13. Richard Tren, "Greenpeace – Black Deaths," Africa Fighting Malaria website, May 2003 (www.fightingmalaria.org).

Radical Environmentalism's Annual Toll
Developing country illness and death attributable in part to ideological environmentalism — a partial global summary

DEATHS	
Dysentery and diarrhea	3,000,000 children
	1,000,000 adults
Malaria	900,000 infants & children
	1,000,000 adults
Malnutrition	3,000,000 infants, children & adults
Measles, diptheria & tetanus	3,000,000 infants & children
Pneumonia and other	4,000,000 infants & children
respiratory diseases	1,000,000 adults, mainly women
Typhus	500,000 infants, children & adults
Vitamin A Deficiency-related	2,000,000 children
Babies (all causes)	5,000,000 dead in their first month
TOTAL annual deaths	20,000,000 infants, children & adults
SUB-LETHAL	
Malnutrition	120,000,000 infants, children & adults
Vitamin A Deficiency	500,000 children blinded

(Sources: World Health Organization, UNICEF, World Bank and others, 2001)

7

Renewable Energy Mirages

Paeans to renewable energy have long been a staple mantra of the ideological environmental movement. It's free. It's forever. It's non-polluting. It's from little entrepreneurs, not from multinational Big Oil companies.

But where does the romantic promise, the never-ending hype over renewable energy end – and the reality begin?

During the six-year period between 1997 and 2002, BP invested some $200 million in solar power. The company claims it will expand this into a billion-dollar business by 2007. Worldwide, it currently generates a combined total of 77 megawatts (MW) of wind and solar power, Cait Murphy noted in *Fortune*.[1] These numbers and the company's ad campaign make its commitment to renewable energy sound quite impressive. However:

> • BP's 77 MW of solar and wind output is barely enough to keep Boise, Idaho's lights lit for a year. By contrast, its oil and natural gas production (3.4 billion barrels of oil

equivalent, or BOE in 2001) could satisfy all of America's oil needs for six months.[2]
• Wind and solar energy producton throughout the world currently provides only 0.1 percent of global primary energy production.[3]
• BP became the world's "largest producer of solar energy" primarily by spending $45 million to buy the Solarex Corporation.[4] That's 0.05 percent of what it spent to buy Arco and Amoco, or 0.9 percent of what it intends to spend between 2002 and 2006 on oil exploration in Alaska.
• During 2001 alone, BP spent $8.5 billion exploring for and producing oil and gas. Its average annual investment of $33.3 million in solar thus amounts to an almost imperceptible 0.4 percent of its 2001 petroleum expenditures.[5]

Even BP's Chief Executive Officer, Lord John Browne, admits that the company's press releases, wall ads and investments will not take it "beyond petroleum" for at least 20 years. Until then, he confessed to executives attending the June 2003 World Gas Conference, "hydrocarbons will not just remain the most important source of energy – they will actually become more important." In fact, all the renewable energy produced today across the entire planet, excluding hydroelectric power, "would barely meet" Tokyo's needs, he noted. Even in 2020 and beyond, "65 percent [of the world's energy] will come from oil and gas."[6]

BP's rapidly escalating oil and gas investments should therefore not be surprising. After all, BP is, first and foremost, a British *Petroleum* company. Its investment decisions thus reflect what its managers, engineers, scientists and economists determine are likely to be the most promising – and the most profitable – technologies for the near and mid term. And Bigger Profits will depend on oil and natural gas, not wind or solar.

Of course, these inconvenient facts do not seem to have gotten in the way of the company's advertising hyperbole. Neither have the environmental, economic and practical downsides of politically correct renewable energy.

Renewables will eventually play an important role in our energy mix. The electricity they generate is much more expensive than fossil, hydro or nuclear versions, but it is still a welcome addition to many power grids. However, managerial decisions, ad campaigns and taxpayer financial outlays need to reflect more hard reality, and less romanticism, hype and deception.

Wind power continues to be promoted as a viable, earth-friendly energy source, from Oregon and California to Wisconsin and Massachusetts. Indeed, the American Wind Energy Association claims the United States could generate 20 percent of its electricity by dedicating "less than 1 percent" of its landmass to wind farms. That sounds mighty attractive to a lot of people, many of whom might see wind turbines as an excellent way to replace the 20 percent of our electricity that now comes from nuclear power plants.[7]

However, 1 percent of the US is 23,000,000 acres – the entire state of Virginia. Covering this much land with tall, noisy wind turbines is hardly an earth-friendly or sustainable alternative to fossil fuels. (By contrast, the nuclear power plants that provide 20 percent of America's electricity together utilize roughly 73,000 acres.[8]) To be effective, these wind-driven eyesores would have to sit atop ridges, hills and escarpments, becoming a glaring visual blight across vast scenic vistas. To be economically viable, journalist Ronald Bailey points out, they depend on government tax breaks and mandates that *require* utilities to produce a certain percentage of their electricity from "renewable" sources.[9]

Wind turbines kill thousands of raptors and other birds annually – an ecological impact that would likely bring any proposal for a fossil fuel power plant to a screeching halt. The National Audubon Society initiated a campaign to stop construction of a wind power farm near Los Angeles, because many birds, including endangered condors, were threatened by the huge turbines. "It is hard to imagine a worse idea than putting a condor Cuisinart next door to critical condor habitat," Audubon's Daniel Beard commented at the time.[10]

Wind turbines work only when the wind is blowing at certain speeds. Because they're not operating much of the time, their actual output hovers at 35 percent of their rated capacity, and can go much lower. When the wind stops blowing, they produce no energy. Thus, even with a forest of giant wind turbines, communities would still need expensive gas-fired power plants, standing idle much of the time but ready to provide instantaneous substitute or supplemental electricity to ensure the continued operation of businesses, schools, factories, homes and essential services like police and fire departments, traffic lights, water treatment plants and hospitals.

Gas-fired plants also require far less land than do wind farms. A gas-fired power plant capable of generating 50 megawatts of electricity typically requires 5-10 acres of land, compared with up to 10,000 acres for a wind facility of similar capacity.

Britain's planned Welsh wind farm of 39 turbines (Europe's largest) will have a total rated capacity of just 60 megawatts. At a more realistic 18 MW output (35 percent of rated capacity), 4,500 of these 400-foot-tall behemoths would be needed to "replace" a single 2,000 MW coal- or gas-fired power plant, says Dr. S. Fred Singer, emeritus professor of environmental sciences at the University of Virginia.[11]

Recent events suggest that even ideological environ-mentalists support renewable energy only as long as it is a theoretical substitute for detested fossil fuels. Once a theoretical choice becomes an actual proposal, support evaporates. In Massachusetts, for example, pro-renewable energy sentiments were transformed almost overnight into "gale-force indignation," when Cape Wind Associates proposed a wind farm off the Cape Cod coast. Walter Cronkite, the Kennedy clan and other upper-crust "Not-On-My-Beachfront" wind-energy promoters were aghast at the thought of enormous, ugly wind turbines interfering with their sail boats and disturbing the scenic serenity of their ocean vistas.[12]

Much the same reaction occurs when someone proposes to build a geothermal energy plant, since most of the good US thermal sites are near scenic natural areas like Yellowstone, Lassen or Hawaii Volcanoes National Park.

Solar power is also land intensive. The more power desired, the more land required. A 50 MW photovoltaic operation involves blanketing well over 1,000 acres with solar panels and access roads to maintain and clean them (assuming an optimistic 10 W/m2 or 5 percent peak efficiency), observes Kenneth Davis, former deputy secretary for the US Department of Energy. Using the sun to meet California's electricity needs would mean paving over hundreds of thousands of acres of desert habitat – along with their resident plant and animal life.[13]

Like wind power, solar also requires expensive gas-fired backup electrical generators, for nighttime and cloudy days. Of course, placing solar or photovoltaic panels on houses and other buildings, to offset some or all of their electricity or heating needs, does not create these ecological problems and should be encouraged. However, such systems cannot possibly begin to meet the electrical or other energy needs of a modern urban community. Large-scale solar arrays, on the other hand, are simply too variable, too unreliable and too ecologically damaging to make more than a minor contribution for many decades to come.

Hydrogen (H_2) may be abundant, but separating it from other molecules is expensive, and takes more energy than is generated by running pure hydrogen through fuel cells. Per unit of heat generated, more CO_2 is produced by making H_2 from fossil fuels than by burning the fuels directly.[14] Ironically, some have proposed that nuclear power plants be built to generate electricity by day and produce hydrogen molecules by night.[15]

It's a chicken-and-egg problem. "We cannot have large numbers of fuel-cell vehicles without adequate fuel available to support them," note several General Motors' hydrogen fuel-cell development experts, "but we will not be able to create the required infrastructure unless there are significant numbers of fuel-cell vehicles on the roadways."[16]

America has a trillion-dollar infrastructure in place for its gasoline-powered automotive fleet. Replacing it with an effective system for distributing and serving up hydrogen is a daunting engineering and economic challenge, making any hydrogen-fueled transportation system a very expensive and thus highly unlikely prospect in the absence of massive tax incentives.[17] Fuel cells based on *gasoline*, on the other hand, would use the nation's existing infrastructure and enable cars to increase their mileage, and reduce their tailpipe emissions, significantly and at far lower cost.

Getting hydrogen into cars is also a challenge. A single tank of gasoline contains 2 million Btus of energy. A five-gallon propane tank full of hydrogen at 150 psi holds only 7,000 Btu – meaning 285 barbecue tanks would be needed to equal a tank of gasoline.[18] That's a daunting task, even for a huge SUV. Heavier high-pressure containers of liquefied hydrogen could reduce the space requirement to about the volume of an average car trunk, but this would wipe out cargo space and spark fears of "Hindenburgian" conflagrations, if a container ruptured in a collision.

(Of course, the possibility of such a conflagration is probably remote, because of the way fuel tanks are constructed. However, tort lawyers and precautionary principle aficionados will certainly ponder them carefully.)

Biomass is another favorite "substitute" for despised fossil fuels. In fact, none other than Shell Oil plans to grow trees on "sustainably" managed plantations, solely to burn them to generate electricity. It claims planting new trees will generate photosynthesis and absorb the carbon dioxide liberated during combustion, thereby preventing hypothetical global warming.

Lewis Carroll and Jonathon Swift would have delighted at exploring how a reversion to wood fires represents "progress" in an age of nuclear power. They'd have even more fun discussing the sanity of radical environmentalists who oppose using any carbon-based fuel except "biomass," and become livid at the thought of cutting even diseased or burned trees (except perhaps if solar-powered chain saws alone were used, and if no one made a profit off the logging).[19]

On the other hand, one form of biomass merits serious consideration and, indeed, has become a vital electrical source in many US communities. Modern waste-to-energy (WTE) plants burn household garbage to generate electricity, while emitting almost no pollution. As an added bonus, they can also increase recycling rates and reduce trash collection and recycling costs – by turning hard to recycle trash into electricity and recovering even paper clips, staples, metal lightbulb and canister bottoms, and other recyclable items that otherwise would end up in landfills.

The United States generates some 225 million tons of trash each year, burning over 40 million tons of it in 120 WTE plants in 30 states. These facilities help serve the waste disposal needs of 40 million Americans, generating 2,800 megawatts of electricity in the process – enough for 2.5 million homes. Fairfax County, Virginia alone burns 1.1 million tons of garbage every year, generating enough electricity to meet the needs of 75,000 homes that otherwise would have to depend on oil, natural gas, coal or nuclear power. But by burning trash, the county is able to conserve 70 million gallons of fuel oil or 370,000 tons of coal every year – and reduce by 90 percent the amount of trash that has to go to landfills.[20]

Too much, or too little energy – that is the question. Even if all the environmental problems associated with fossil and nuclear power could be solved, one suspects that radical environmentalists would still be unhappy. Their real gripe appears to be that nuclear and fossil fuels actually do what they were designed to do: provide reliable, affordable, abundant energy.

> • "It'd be a little short of disastrous for us to discover a source of clean, cheap, abundant energy because of what we would do with it," says soft energy advocate Amory Lovins. "We ought to be looking for energy sources that are adequate for our needs, but won't give us the excesses of concentrated energy with which we could do mischief to the Earth or to each other."[21]
> • "Giving society cheap, abundant energy would be the equivalent of giving an idiot child a machine gun," argues doom-and-gloom prognosticator Paul Ehrlich.[22]

But real experts recognize the vital, fundamental role that energy plays in modern society.

> • "A reliable and affordable supply of energy is absolutely critical to maintaining and expanding economic prosperity where such prosperity already exists, and to creating it where it does not," emphasizes Dr. John Holdren, Professor of Environmental Policy at Harvard University.[23]
> • "Reliable and affordable access to modern energy services is an indicator of sustainable development," the World Energy Council has stated, "for without it basic needs cannot be satisfied."[24]

The "triple bottom line" here is really quite simple.

First, renewable energy is not yet ready for prime time. Not only is it highly misleading to tell investors, consumers and policy makers that it is ready now, or that it's just around the corner. Doing so also results in horrendous tax, economic, investment and public policy decisions.

Second, the environmental case for renewables erroneously assumes that: wind and solar facilities are sustainable and ecologically benign; burning fossil fuels causes global warming; and fossil fuels are rapidly being depleted. In fact, the environmental impacts of wind and solar energy are numerous and significant. By contrast, the frightening tales about catastrophic global climate change are based on computer models and activist scare-mongering – and have no basis in scientific evidence, as Chapter 8 makes clear.

As to exhausting the world's fossil fuel supplies, that day may eventually come. But it is much farther in the future than green activists care to admit, as is clear from data compiled by Dr. Robert Bradley, Jr. of the Institute for Energy Research.

> • In 1947, the world's proven reserves of crude oil totaled only 68 billion barrels. Over the next 50 years, we consumed 783 billion barrels – and at the end of 1998 still had proven reserves of 1,050 billion barrels! Back in 1966, the world had proven natural gas reserves of just 1,040 trillion cubic feet (tcf). By the end of 1998, we had used up 1,880 tcf – and still had untapped reserves of 5,145 tcf!
> • At 1998 consumption rates, today's proven reserves are equal to 43 years of oil and 62 years of natural gas – and crews are still finding new deposits all over the world.[25] In fact, vast areas of our planet remain unexplored, due to technological, terrain, weather, political and other factors.

The notion that we are rapidly exhausting energy (and metal) resources also reflects an abysmal grasp of basic mineral economic principles. "Proven reserves" is not a static number. It reflects what we need and can expect to extract from known deposits at a particular commodity price and with existing technology. As more deposits are discovered, prices increase, and technologies improve, proven reserve numbers also rise, often dramatically.

In May 2003, to cite just one example, Canada increased its proven oil reserve figures from 4 billion barrels to 180 billion barrels! Almost overnight and with the stroke of a pen, it became a global petroleum powerhouse, behind only Saudi Arabia and Iraq in total reserves. Canada was able to do this simply by recognizing that, even at just $15 per barrel, many of its vast tar sand reserves were commercially and technologically producible.

Overcoming political obstacles to finding and developing deposits in the Arctic National Wildlife Refuge, US Outer Continental Shelf and other prospects will also increase proven petroleum reserves. Meanwhile, improved fuel cell, hybrid vehicle, nuclear, coal, biotech, pollution control and other technologies will greatly stretch the life of existing fossil fuel and uranium deposits.

One must also hope that wind and solar power will eventually play a more prominent role than today. Of course, this means ways must be found to store energy generated when the wind is blowing and the sun is shining – and to resolve land use, bird kill and other environmental problems.

Moreover, our creative genius will continue to develop new technologies that few of us can even conceive of today – any more than people living in 1904 could have imagined the amazing technologies we take for granted today. These breakthroughs and changing societal needs will constantly alter the kinds and amounts of energy, metallic and non-metallic resources we require. At the same time, ongoing innovative efforts will continue to promote the vital, though less dramatic progress that transforms our energy and raw material needs on an almost daily basis.

Because of incremental improvements in extrusion technology, aluminum beverage cans are now 30 percent lighter than they were in the 1960s, greatly reducing the amount of metal needed to make a billion cans. Improvements in tensile strength and architectural design mean modern high-rise buildings require 35 percent less steel than did their counterparts a mere 20 years ago. Today, a single fiber-optic cable made from 60 pounds of silica sand (the most abundant element on earth) carries hundreds of times more information than did an "old-fashioned" cable made from 2,000 pounds of copper, technological eons ago in the 1980s.[26] Wireless technologies will continue to reduce raw material needs.

Third and most important, for Northern Hemisphere NGOs and policy makers to tell Third World nations that they must rely on wind and solar power – and forego hydroelectric, nuclear or fossil fuel projects – is to deprive the world's poorest citizens of reliable, affordable energy. It condemns billions of people to continued poverty and misery. And it does so for no valid reason – but only to promote the ideologies of vocal activists whose indifference to this abject poverty and early death will eventually prove their undoing.

Chapter Seven Footnotes

1. Cait Murphy, "Is BP Beyond Petroleum? Hardly," *Fortune*, September 30, 2002.
2. *Ibid.*
3. Energy Information Administration, *International Energy Annual 1999: World Energy Overview*; Ronald Bailey, *Global Warming and Other Eco-Myths: How the environmental movement uses false science to scare us to death*, Washington, DC: Competitive Enterprise Institute (2002), pages 250-260; Bjorn Lomborg, *The Skeptical Environmentalist: Measuring the real state of the world*, Cambridge University Press (2001), page 130.
4. Kenny Bruno, "A convenient confusion," *New Internationalist 335*, June 2001.
5. *Ibid.*
6. Lord John Browne, "The Strategic Role of Gas," keynote speech delivered at the 22nd World Gas Conference in Tokyo, Japan, June 2, 2003. See also Cait Murphy, *op. cit.*, noting that BP regional president Bob Malone said much the same thing in mid-2002.
7. "Farming the wind," *Parade* magazine, June 23, 2002. See also "Wind power costly, consultant says," *Charleston, WV Gazette-Mail*, December 3, 2002.
8. Nuclear Energy Institute, personal communication, September 6, 2002.
9. See Ronald Bailey, "Wind Breaks: Why the favorite energy resource of environmental activists is unsustainable," www.sepp.org/newSEPP/WindBreaks-RonaldBailey.htm
10. *National Review, The Week*, October 11, 1999.
11. S. Fred Singer, "Will UK get towers of power ... or a load of hot air?" *Environment & Climate News*, September 2002.
12. Collin Levey, "Tilting at windmills" [in Nantucket Sound], *Wall Street Journal*, August 8, 2002. One of the most prominent critics of the Massachusetts offshore wind farm is John F. Kennedy, Jr., who on several occasions refused to tell radio host Sean Hannity how he can be such a strong wind and solar proponent, and yet be so adamantly opposed to a *bona fide* wind project.
13. W. Kenneth Davis, "The coming electric power crisis: A think piece," *The Week That Was*, Science and Environmental Policy Project, November 25, 2000; Paul Driessen, "Recipe for Disaster: What really caused the California energy crisis? What can we do now?" Committee For A Constructive Tomorrow (www.CFACT.org), April 2001. However, new approaches to wind and solar technology, such as that being developed by Pyron Solar of San Diego, CA (www.PyronSolar.com), will continue to drive innovative approaches for renewable power.

14. Martin I. Hoffert, Thomas Wigley, et al., "Advanced Technology Paths to Global Climate Stability: Energy for a Greenhouse Planet," *Science*, November 1, 2002; vol. 298; pages 981-987
15. "The burning question of hydrogen," editorial, *Washington Times*, November 10, 2002.
16. Lawrence D. Burns, J. Byron McCormick and Christopher E. Borroni-Bird, "Vehicle of Change: Hydrogen-fuel-cell cars could be the catalyst for a cleaner tomorrow," *Scientific American*, October 2002. See also article by Ralph Kinney Bennett, "The ICE Age Isn't Over," TechCentralStation.com, June 18, 2003 (ICE = internal combustion engine).
17. At this time, there is but one place in the world where a hydrogen-fueled car can be refueled: Hamburg, Germany's international airport.
18. Jim Hood, letter to the editor, *Washington Times*, November 12, 2002.
19. John McCaslin, "Solar sawing," TownHall.com, July 2, 2002. Air pollution from wood burning stoves and fire places (soot, hydrocarbons and carbon dioxide) is a serious problem, according to the US Environmental Protection Agency. Under pressure from the EPA, California has proposed banning such heat sources and requiring some 500,000 homeowners to permanently disable their fireplaces and stoves, converting them to natural gas or upgrading them to modern systems with soot scrubbers, before they can sell their homes. Anyone caught burning wood on "bad air days" could be fined. "Fireplace owners smoking: California area ban considered," *The Washington Times*, December 10, 2002. The proposal raises fascinating questions for civil libertarians, anti-fossil-fuel zealots, pro-renewable alarmists, sustainable development aficionados and global warming catastrophists alike.
20. Margaret Charles and Jonathon Kiser, "Waste to Energy: Benefits beyond waste disposal," *Solid Waste Technologies, 1995 Industry Sourcebook*; Ogden Martin Systems of Fairfax (now Coventa Energy), "The I-95 Energy/Resource Recovery Facility," 1999. The use of genetic engineering in industrial processes, however, promises reduced air and water pollution, expanded production of new bio-fuels from corn stalks and other waste materials, and reductions in the amounts of energy and raw materials required in manufacturing processes. See "Saving the world in comfort," *The Economist*, March 27, 2003 (editorial); *New Biotech Tools for a Cleaner Environment; Industrial biotechnology for pollution prevention, resource conservation and cost reduction*, Washington, DC: Biotechnology Industry Organization (2004); and *Plants for the Future*, Brussels: European Commission office of Energy Research (2004). Eco-friendly technologies, however, must still convince GM opponents.

98   **Eco-Imperialism**

21. Amory Lovins, "The Mother Earth," *Playboy* interview, November-December 1977.
22. Paul Ehrlich, "An Ecologist's Perspective on Nuclear Power," Federation of American Scientists, *Public Issue Report*, May-June 1978. Ehrlich's gloomy predictions have never proven correct, but his comments continue to command media attention.
23. John Holdren, "Memorandum to the President: The Energy-Climate Challenge," in Donald Kennedy and John Riggs, editors, *US Policy and the Global Environment: Memos to the President* (Washington, DC: The Aspen Institute, 2000), page 21.
24. World Energy Council, *Living in One World*, London: World Energy Council (2001), page 74.
25. Robert L. Bradley, Jr., *Julian Simon and the Triumph of Energy Sustainability*, Washington, DC: American Legislative Exchange Council (2000), pages 28-35. An emerging school of geological thought maintains that not all petroleum may be of organic origin, but is being formed continually by tectonic and other forces from carbon and hydrogen deep inside the earth.
26. Lynn Scarlett and Jane Shaw, *Environmental Progress: What every executive should know*, Bozeman, MT: Political Economy Research Center (1999); Lynn Scarlett, "Doing More with Less: De-materialization – unsung environmental triumph?" in Ronald Bailey (editor), *Earth Report 2000: Revisiting the True State of the Planet*, New York: McGraw-Hill (2000).

8

Climate Change Riches

The very definition of corporate social responsibility – to say nothing of its actual implementation – raises an entire new genre of far-reaching concerns. Not just for businesses, but for families, communities and nations. The world's poorest citizens are especially vulnerable.

How corporations respond to the challenge will play a critical role in determining whether our future will be shaped by science, technology, freedom and hope – or driven by junk science, eco-imperialism and fear. Many of the omens do not engender optimism.

In May 1997, British Petroleum CEO John Browne endorsed the catastrophic global warming hypothesis and said tough measures should be taken quickly, even without scientific proof. Many interpreted BP's support for the precautionary principle as evidence that the company was convinced about the science and had decided to become a "responsible citizen."[1] Indeed, Sir John later said, "We accepted that the risks were serious and that precautionary action was justified. We were the first company in our industry to do so, and the first to say that, if we were asking other people to take precautionary action, we had to show what was possible and to set an example."[2]

Under the leadership of chairman Sir Mark Moody-Stuart, Royal Dutch/Shell likewise played a lead role in promoting CSR, sustainable development, the precautionary principle and the Kyoto Protocol on climate change. The company issued a series of reports on "people, planet and profits," offering guidance on the meaning and purpose of CSR, the nature of the corporate commitment it requires, and how companies should actually implement its doctrines.[3]

Only rarely have these companies or any other members of the World Business Council for Sustainable Development suggested that NGO opinions, CSR assumptions or global warming theories might be ill-informed, misleading, false or even open to question. Nor have they opined that their perverse definitions of corporate social responsibility and precaution might actually be harmful to millions of people.

Indeed, BP, Shell and other WBC members provide significant financial and political support for activists, politicians and regulators to further promote CSR and global warming agendas. They are also strong proponents of the notion that CSR principles and global warming theories are "widely accepted" and "irrefutable" – permitting little disagreement or deviation.

According to the Shell-BP-WBC-EU line of thinking, neither companies, communities nor countries should be able to adopt their own definition of corporate social responsibility, sustainable development, the precautionary principle or climate risk – to fit their own unique circumstances, their own pressing needs and priorities, or their own assessment of available scientific evidence. To permit this, they seem to believe, would "tilt the playing field," give some an "unfair advantage," and result in irresponsible or unethical practices.

When it comes to pursuing profits from global warming and "emission trading" schemes, however, some have suggested that BP is in a class by itself – surpassing even Enron, and with Shell close behind. These schemes involve trading money or other valuable commodities for the right to emit greenhouse gases. They would go into effect once the Kyoto treaty is implemented, and nations and companies are forced to switch from coal to natural gas in manufacturing and electrical power generation (or else reduce productive capacity and industrial output), to combat theoretical catastrophic global climate change.

Columnist Robert Novak brought to light several internal Enron memos that outlined in detail how the company believed it could parlay the Kyoto treaty into immensely profitable business endeavors. A December 12, 1997 memo asserted that Enron had "excellent credentials" with many environmental groups that, the memo claimed, referred to Enron "in glowing terms." It argued that the Kyoto treaty would "do more to promote Enron's business" than any other initiative and said the treaty's emissions trading authority would be "good for Enron stock!!"

An August 4, 1997 memo to Enron president Ken Lay sought to prepare him for a White House meeting on how to persuade the United States to embrace the climate treaty. Present at the meeting were President Clinton, Vice President Gore and BP CEO Sir John Browne. The memo described BP as Enron's "international equivalent," presumably because of the UK giant's global reach, similar policy objectives and generally good reputation among environmental groups.[4]

Sir John "thinks there will soon be government regulation of greenhouse gases. And companies that have anticipated regulation will not only know how to use it to their advantage; they will also, as Browne puts it, 'gain a seat at the table, a chance to influence future rules.'"[5]

The United States Senate, Bush Administration, many American companies and numerous scientists, on the other hand, have vigorously objected to the treaty. They point out that climate change science and theories are still being hotly debated; computer models are still far too primitive to analyze complex weather systems or predict future climate changes accurately; and the treaty is likely to devastate many countries' economies, while generating few, if any environmental benefits.

More than 18,000 scientists (including hundreds of weather and climate experts) have signed a petition sponsored by the Oregon Institute of Science and Medicine, saying they see "no convincing evidence" that humans are disrupting the earth's climate. We simply do not know enough about what drives climate fluctuations, they emphasize, and available evidence simply doesn't support the terrifying "Frankenclime" horror movie scenarios that dominate television and newspaper headlines.[6]

As to computer models, they don't begin to reflect climate or atmospheric complexities. Worse, they disagree with observed temperature data, cannot accurately predict future or replicate past temperatures, and produce wildly contradictory projections for the very same regions. Worst, they incorporate absurd assumptions about future economic growth and emissions. One United Nations scenario, for example, projects that Libya and North Korea will have higher per capita incomes than the United States by the end of this century, Steve Forbes has pointed out.[7]

About the only point on which computer models and observed temperature data agree is this: Any planetary warming is most likely to occur in the Earth's coldest, driest regions (Alaska and Siberia), at night, in mid-winter. But of course, even if these areas were to warm by 5 degrees (from minus 20 to minus 15, for instance), the amount of glacial melting caused by this "catastrophic" global warming will be negligible – and the warmer winter temperatures would be welcomed by local residents.

Scientists also note that global temperatures have *not* been increasing, and that historical evidence and objective data strongly suggest that the earth was warmer during the Middle Ages than it is today. After examining 1,000 years of global temperature data and more than 240 scientific journals from the past 40 years, scientists from the Harvard-Smithsonian Center for Astrophysics concluded that current average temperatures are some 2 degrees lower than during the "medieval warm period," which lasted from about 900 to 1300 AD and was followed by a "little ice age" from 1300 to 1850. After that, average worldwide temperatures again warmed slightly (about 1 degree) until around 1970, when the planet began to cool slightly, before warming slightly again.[8]

Planet Earth is currently enjoying a warm "interglacial period" – part of a natural cycle of balmy climate, interrupted by far longer stretches of mile-deep ice packs across Europe and North America. The pattern has gone on now for some 800,000 years, in roughly 100,000-year cycles. If, as the evidence clearly suggests, all these fluctuations are within the realm of natural variability, all the consternation over "man-induced" climate change is clearly misplaced. Even worse, it may cause us to impose costly, draconian measures that we will soon regret.

A recent report by the US National Aeronautics and Space Administration suggests that increases in solar radiation, during sometimes-prolonged periods of quiet sunspot activity, could also be a principal cause of climate change. "Historical records of solar

activity indicate that solar radiation has been increasing since the late 19th century," says lead author Richard Wilson. If sustained over many decades, such trends "could cause significant climate change."[9]
Unfortunately, many studies are being politicized. "Science, in the public arena, is commonly used as a source of authority with which to bludgeon political opponents and propagandize uninformed citizens," says atmospheric physicist Richard S. Lindzen. "This is what has been done with both the reports of the IPCC and NAS [Intergovernmental Panel on Climate Change and National Academy of Sciences]. It is a reprehensible practice that corrodes our ability to make rational decisions. A fairer view of the science will show that there is still a vast amount of uncertainty – far more than advocates of Kyoto would like to acknowledge."[10]
Climate alarmists have found that they can dramatically alter the scientific findings, by drafting "summaries" and press releases that emotionalize the issues and tilt the findings in favor of their agenda. But why would they engage in such sleight-of-hand ethics? "To capture the public imagination," climate scientist, global warming activist and former global cooling prophet Stephen Schneider once said, "we have to offer up some scary scenarios, make simplified dramatic statements, and make little mention of any doubts we might have. Each of us has to decide what the right balance is between being effective and being honest."[11]
Available evidence simply does not support alarmist climate theory. To let activist policy agendas replace scientific integrity is neither socially responsible nor in anyone's best interest.

However, despite extensive evidence that global warming is nothing more than a frightening theory, the Kyoto climate treaty would compel signatory nations to reduce fossil fuel use and greenhouse gas emissions, in many cases by virtually impossible amounts. The United States, for example, would have to slash its fossil fuel use to some 40 percent below what it would otherwise be by 2012. That's almost a 25 percent reduction from current energy use levels.
The US Energy Information Administration has calculated that the treaty could drain over $300 billion a year from a US economy that drives one-third of the entire global economy. Energy prices would go up by 50 percent or more, and millions of American

jobs would be lost, making it even more difficult for trade-dependant developing countries to climb out of poverty. The climate treaty's impact on Canada, Europe, Japan and Australia would be similarly devastating, further harming developing nations, and stifling technological and scientific advancement.

Such widespread economic harm would also lead to significant environmental damage. As Indira Gandhi once remarked, "Poverty is the worst polluter." Wealthy countries have the time, motivation, technology and financial ability to address ecological concerns. Third World nations do not.

Developing countries like China and India are thus hardly likely to sacrifice their future economic growth on the altar of eco-political correctitude. Russia too has begun to recognize that its recent 7 percent annual economic growth rates would suffer, if it signs the Kyoto treaty. These nations are likely to continue burning cheap, plentiful coal (hopefully with improved air pollution controls), to generate electricity and assure a better future for their people. So global greenhouse gas emissions will continue to rise, no matter what today's developed nations might do.

As a result, all the developed world's economic misery would bring few benefits. In fact, according to the National Center for Atmospheric Research, even "full and perfect compliance" with Kyoto would reduce average global temperatures in 2050 by only 0.13°F below what they would be in the treaty's absence. Actually stabilizing "greenhouse gases" at current concentrations would require "19 Kyotos" – reducing global emissions to at least 60 percent below *1990* levels, even as the sun's energy output continues to fluctuate, and emissions rise in developing countries that are not subject to the treaty's requirements. This would drive US use of fossil fuels downward to Depression Era levels.[12]

The painful reality is that no carbon-free energy technology exists on a scale that could stabilize or reduce global carbon dioxide levels. Nuclear and hydroelectric power could help, but neither technology is high on the radical greens' list of "appropriate" technologies. Wind and solar could likewise make a contribution, if the world were willing to sacrifice scenic vistas, bird populations, desert habitats and modern standards of living to these intermittent energy producers.

However, where some see economic chaos, others see opportunity. In its heyday, Enron envisioned billions of dollars in new revenue. Today BP, various European countries and others believe they can create and run a complex system intended to ensure that they will do well economically and politically, while others wallow in social and economic misery.

Profits can be a strong incentive to support dire forecasts of ecological Armageddon. At least some of the supposedly principled, altruistic, moral concern about global warming on the part of BP, Shell and other companies may actually be motivated by little more than a crass desire to develop new revenue streams and maximize profits.

BP for example has a substantial and growing stake in natural gas, which many tout as a principal substitute for coal and oil, since it emits less carbon dioxide when burned. (One unit of energy produced by gas results in a third less carbon dioxide than if the energy source is oil, and one-half as much compared to coal.) Ratification of the Kyoto accords would send the value of BP's gas holdings skyward, significantly improving its bottom line – the traditional one, as well as the fabled "triple bottom line."

A second motivator might be emissions trading. Before it went belly-up in Chapter 11, "Enron hoped to cash in on Kyoto by masterminding a worldwide trading network in which major industries could buy and sell credits to emit carbon dioxide," observes Bill O'Keefe, president of the George Marshall Institute.[13] BP may now be in a position to replace Enron as the primary power broker for any greenhouse gas emissions trading scheme that may emerge from the climate change debates, as nations seek to find ways to comply with its draconian provisions, without decimating their industries and economies.[14]

Credits that now sell for a few cents or couple dollars per ton of emissions might go for $10, $20 or $100 a ton under a mandatory Kyoto program. This would clearly generate tremendous returns on investment – and a huge incentive for these "socially responsible" companies to get on the global warming bandwagon and promote "vigorous action to combat catastrophic global climate change." Some analysts have predicted that the global market for emission credits could grow to nearly $2 trillion by 2025![15]

A proposed European Emissions Trading Directive would enable countries that are not part of the European Union to link their programs with those of the EU, and thus recognize and trade in each other's allowances. The directive is also intended as a practice run, giving EU nations and companies experience and a competitive advantage, before the Kyoto treaty comes into full force in 2008 (if it is indeed ratified, despite continued reluctance on the part of the United States, Canada, Australia and Russia).

At Sir John Browne's direction, BP has already set up a corporate emissions trading system, "in which each of its 150 business units, spread across more than 100 countries, would be assigned a quota of emissions permits and encouraged to trade with one another."[16] The BP system could thus aid in the design of a much broader program, and give the company a competitive edge in designing and coordinating a European or even global system, should it choose to seek such a role.

The potential for fraud and other mischief is enormous, as is the potential for unscrupulous companies (and countries) to get wealthy from the prospect of others' economic misery.

Russia's CO_2 emissions are some 35 percent below its 1990, pre-USSR-collapse levels. This could be a valuable source of revenue, particularly if Russia holds out for major monetary concessions, as its price for ratifying Kyoto and foregoing much of its own economic future. The Kremlin could sell billions of euros of emissions credits to nations that exceed their Kyoto targets. Europe will also be dependent on Russian natural gas to provide for economic growth, putting Russia in an enviable position versus the EU.

But both Russia and other participating nations could engage in much sleight-of-hand. What, for instance, is to prevent games of Let's pretend? As in: "We were thinking about building a huge coal-burning factory. But if you'll pay us $1 billion for the CO_2 it would have emitted, we won't build it, and you can build the plants that Kyoto otherwise prohibits, because you have already exceeded your permissible emissions allowance."

There are no systems in place to measure, verify or police actual, potential or mythical emissions from the vast array of stationary and mobile GHG sources, notes O'Keefe. No standards exist to regulate these transactions – comparable to what have long governed US commodity trading and accounting practices. With emission trading, it's "an open invitation for fraud and abuse. How much easier will it be to cook the emissions books for an international system, when the measurement standards and means to verify emission reductions are yet to be developed, tested and verified?"[17]

Global warming research is also a lucrative business, with the promise of life-long careers and research grants. The White House alone spent some $18 billion on global warming research and "education" between 1992 and 2000, during the Clinton-Gore administration. The United Nations spent billions more, as did the European Union. The Pew Charitable Trusts gave $5 million to its Global Climate Change Center in 2000, and the International Institute for Sustainable Development is spending $700,000 just to assess "how farmers in India may be vulnerable" to problems supposedly due to "economic globalization and climate change." The vast bulk of this money went to researchers who support basic catastrophic global warming hypotheses.

Dr. Stephen Pecala is a Princeton University researcher working under a $20-million BP-funded grant. In response to questions after his formal address at a 2002 oil industry conference on global climate change, he suggested that oil companies should embrace the Kyoto Protocol and global climate change theories, because they could raise their per-barrel prices through a self-imposed energy tax. The tax would promote greenhouse gas sequestration and would allow companies to reap the *full* benefits of oil development, he argued.

In other words, energy and other companies that play the climate change game according to the Kyoto rules could earn billions of dollars in profits via traditional steps of petroleum extraction, refining and sales – and then "earn" billions more by disposing of the resultant carbon via emission trading and sequestration schemes.[18]

Power and influence also motivate. Western Europe clearly wants to protect its industries, preserve its massive welfare state, and successfully integrate the eastern European economic basket case it inherited when the Soviet Union collapsed. Several EU countries also want to serve as a "counterweight" to US interests, as they did over Iraq. Eastern or "new" Europe, meanwhile, wants to bolster its economic growth, make up for decades of forced deprivation, and clean up the serious environmental problems that were ignored during decades of Communism. It has shown less enthusiasm than its "old" Europe counterparts for unproven global warming theories.

Global warming politics also reflect the fact that certain European countries still chafe under American wealth, power and influence that once were theirs, and that they believe should rightfully still be theirs or should be turned over to the United Nations. Climate politics likewise reflect a prevailing green and EU mindset that Americans are crass, greedy, wasteful, and wedded to low-cost energy and "profligate" resource consumption. The United States does use more petroleum per capita than any other nation. However, it also drives a quarter of the global economy, leads the global war against terrorism and feeds starving people worldwide. Despite the demands for fuel that these commitments entail, energy conservation measures saved 78 quads in 2000, compared to what the US would have needed with pre-1973 technology. The measures enabled its economy to grow three times faster than did its energy use between 1973 and 2000. The USA also reduced its pollution significantly. Today's cars, for example, emit less than 1 percent of what 1970 models spewed from their tailpipes.

For nearly two decades, Europe's growth rate has been about half that of the United States, while unemployment has been nearly twice the US rate. Tax burdens in some EU countries are 40 percent or more of their Gross Domestic Product. Europeans seem to prefer high levels of job security, unemployment and welfare – while Americans tend to opt for lower levels, as a tradeoff for greater growth, innovation, living standards, and flexibility in changing jobs and cities. But now some Europeans want to impose their choices as the world's norm.

The EU's self-interest is highly visible in its insistence that Ireland, the United States, Eastern Europe and other nations adopt a system of "global tax equity" or "tax harmonization." This is bureaucratic code for compelling the United States to raise its taxes to EU levels, to prevent "disruption" and eliminate "unfair and harmful tax competition."[19] The concept also raises its ugly head in EU support for the Basel Convention on Transboundary Movement of Hazardous Materials (to protect EU chemical companies and jobs), and in Europe's (mostly France's) intense opposition to GM foods (to protect its agricultural base).

Some suspect that European and green opposition to biotechnology might be related to their insistence that catastrophic climate change is behind every weather oddity and rain, drought or storm cycle. Although droughts are a centuries-old problem in southern Africa, linking the latest ones to global warming might deflect some of the criticism they have received for their antipathy toward GM crops that grow well in saline soils and dry climates. Radical opposition to fossil fuel projects in the Third World might likewise be "justified" by climate change hypotheses. Other claims are far more political in nature. Several major companies and activist groups (including BP, Vivendi, Greenpeace, Friends of the Earth and the World Wildlife Fund) were actually members of the *official* European Commission delegation to the August 2002 Earth Summit in Johannesburg, South Africa! They and Europe in general see the Kyoto Protocol, not merely as an environmental program, but also as a trade issue – another way to pressure the United States to reduce its energy use and economic productivity. That would help bring the US economy down to the level of European nations that refuse to adjust their industrial, labor, tax and welfare policies.

EU Environment Commissioner Margot Wallstroem made precisely this point in response to President Bush's decision to abandon the Kyoto climate treaty. "This is not a simple environmental issue, where you can say it is an issue where the scientists are not unanimous," she declaimed. "This is about international relations, this is about economy, about trying to create a level playing field for big businesses throughout the world. You have to understand what is at stake and that is why it is serious."[20]

Her remarks were echoed by several EU officials, who suggested that America's lower energy taxes constitute an unfair trade advantage that could justify trade sanctions against the US.

The EU countries recognize that they cannot compete with the US or developing countries as long as Europe's tax rates, unemployment levels, welfare benefits and work disincentives remain high; their farms remain mired in traditional or organic practices; their working age populations continue to decline, relative to retirees; and many of their companies are reluctant to become "lean and mean" the way their American counterparts did in the 1980s and 1990s. It is far easier politically for the EU to criticize its competitors, and demand "equitable" arrangements under compulsory international treaties, than to admit and correct its own shortcomings and anti-competitive policies.

The EU, environmental activists and United Nations also envision the Kyoto treaty's restrictions on energy supplies, energy use and greenhouse gas emissions as an opportunity to expand the authority of international institutions. Indeed, French President Jacques Chirac has termed the Kyoto Protocol "the first component of authentic global governance." It would be, moreover, a massive bureaucracy, largely devoid of checks and balances, ensconced primarily in the EU and UN, fed and nourished with billions in tax dollars. The new bureaucracy would hold unprecedented power to control decisions by nations, states, communities, businesses and individuals – over energy, economic, housing, transportation and numerous other matters.[21]

How moral, ethical or socially responsible these corporations are, for promoting their business interests via a climate treaty with such far-reaching impacts, is certainly open to question. How altruistic and socially responsible the EU countries are, for protecting their political and economic interests through the treaty's hidden tariffs, is equally questionable.

It would be far more responsible for companies, governments and foundations alike to take a principled stand in defense of true science, economic improvement, and human life and welfare. Essential first steps include the following.

• Disclose how much money they have provided to activist groups for climate change and other programs.
• Reveal the ways and extent to which they and their activist allies are likely to profit from ratification of the Kyoto climate treaty.
• Insist that further research be undertaken by independent scientists, to determine: whether the Earth's climate is actually changing; how much warming (or cooling) might realistically be expected over the next century; climate change's actual causes (variations in planetary orbits, solar radiation or human emissions); what effects (positive, negative or none) moderate warming might have on the world's environment and agriculture; and what impact severe fossil fuel restrictions would likely have on economic stability and growth, especially for developing countries.
• Publicly challenge catastrophic climate change theories, while actively supporting reasoned and scientifically based debate and action on climate change – and engaging in a

full re-examination of social responsibility, sustainable development and precautionary doctrines.

These modest steps will help ensure that decisions on important public policy matters like global climate change are made on the basis of sound scientific, technological and economic principles, solid empirical evidence, and attention to the needs of the world's poorest citizens. Junk science, activist pressure, corporate intrigue and international power politics would no longer dominate global political processes.

Last but not least, "corporate social responsibility" would regain some of the legitimacy and humanity it lost when radicals hijacked it to serve their anti-business, anti-development, anti-science, anti-people agendas.

Chapter Eight Footnotes

1. Hans Henrik Ramm, "The precautionary principle: A Warning About a New and Alien Political-Scientific Paradigm," Still Waiting for Greenhouse website, December 1997.
2. Sir John Browne, Group Chief Executive of BP, "Beyond Petroleum: Business and the Environment in the 21st Century," to Stanford Graduate School of Business, March 11, 2002. See also Darcy Frey, "How green is BP?" *New York Times Magazine*, December 8, 2002.
3. See *Misguided Virtue*, pages 40-46. Sir Mark is now a member of the board of directors for the "ethical" investor group Innovest Strategic Value Advisors, which recently published two reports: "Intangible values linked to sustainability" and *Value at Risk: Climate Change and the Future of Governance.* Innovest operates the EcoValue'21 analytical platform and includes among its institutional clients several of the world's largest pension funds (CalPERS in the USA, BP in the United Kingdom and ABP in the Netherlands).
4. Robert Novak, "Enron's green side," Townhall.com, January 17, 2002; Chris Horner, "Green with greed," TechCentralStation.com, September 13, 2002; Marc Morano, "Enron and the Clinton Administration: Ties That Bind," *Cybercast News Service,* CNSNews.com, March 18, 2002 (first of a three-part series).
5. Darcy Frey, "How green is BP?"
6. Oregon Petition Project on global warming, Oregon Institute of Science and Medicine, www.oism.org/project. See also the "Still Waiting for Greenhouse" website at http://www.vision.net.au/~daly/
7. Steve Forbes, "We Shall Not Fry," *Forbes*, May 26, 2003. For an excellent, concise, readable summary of current global warming science and economics, see Competitive Enterprise Institute vice president Marlo Lewis's article, "Common Sense," June 4, 2003 – available on www.TechCentralStation.com and from CEI (www.cei.org).
8. Harvard-Smithsonian Center for Astrophysics, "20th Climate Not So Hot," press release, March 31, 2003. The study was published in the spring 2003 *Energy and Environment* journal. See also Wallace Broeker, "Was the Medieval warm period global?" *Science*, Vol. 291, pages 1497-99; Brian Fagan, *The Little Ice Age: The prelude to global warming, 1300-1850*, New York: Basic Books (2000); Paul Driessen and Nick Nichols, "Global Warming: Science versus spin, Capital PR News, Fourth Quarter 2001, http://www.prsa-ncc.org/news/newsLetter.asp?insertPage= NL4Q2001-5.htm. When Erik the Red

colonized Greenland in 980, it really was green, and he was able to grow crops and raise sheep in areas that, by 1400, were covered by ice and snow. Europe then plunged into a 450-year-long "little ice age" that was marked by prolonged rains, floods, crop failures and famines.

9. Krishna Ramanujan, "NASA study finds increasing solar trend that can change climate," news release, Goddard Space Flight Center, Greenbelt, MD, March 20, 2003. For more information about global climate change, and links to additional websites, see www.globalwarming.org; www.sepp.org; Ronald Bailey, *Global Warming and Other Eco-Myths: How the environmental movement uses false science to scare us to death*, Washington, DC: Competitive Enterprise Institute (2002); Bjorn Lomborg, *The Skeptical Environmentalist: Measuring the real state of the world*, Cambridge University Press (2001).

10. Richard Lindzen, "Scientists' report doesn't support the Kyoto treaty," *Wall Street Journal*, June 11, 2001.

11. Jonathan Schell, "Our fragile Earth," *Discover*, October 1987, page 47. In "The Cooling World," the April 28, 1975 issue of *Newsweek* proclaimed that scientists are "almost unanimous" in their concern that an "ominous" cooling trend "will reduce agricultural productivity for the rest of the century" and the world might be heading into another "little ice age."

12. Martin Parry *et al.*, "Adapting to the inevitable," *Nature*, Volume 395, page 741 (1998); Intergovernmental Panel on Climate Change, *Climate Change: The IPCC Scientific Assessment*, Cambridge University Press (1990), and subsequent 1992 and 1995 reports; Energy Information Administration, *Impacts of the Kyoto Protocol on US Energy Markets and Economic Activity* (1998); Margo Thorning, "A Better Way," TechCentralStation.com, November 29, 2002; H. Sterling Burnett, "Kyoto chills hopes of developing world," *Washington Times*, November 18, 2002.

13. William O'Keefe, "Why Enron loved Kyoto, and the EU shouldn't," *Wall Street Journal*, July 25, 2002.

14. See the further discussion of emissions trading in the chapter on "Corporate Social Responsibility." For an examination of economic and political issues facing Europe and the United States, see Margo Thorning, *Climate Change and Public Policy: European and American Approaches to Kyoto*, Washington, DC: Marshall Institute, September 24, 2002.

15. See Brian O'Connell, "Banking on the Apocalypse," *Wall Street Journal Europe,* March 12, 2001. The article notes that Shell, BP, Swiss Re, ICF, Climate Care (UK) and other companies (many of them once strong opponents of the Kyoto agreement) are now "leading the charge for the nascent carbon-trading market."

16. Darcy Frey, "How green is BP?"

17. William O'Keefe, "Why Enron loved Kyoto, and the EU shouldn't."

18. Dr. Stephen W. Pacala, Princeton University, speaking on "Academic & Industry Partnerships/Carbon Mitigation R&D Initiatives," at the Second Annual Climate Change Voluntary Action Conference, sponsored by the American Petroleum Institute, November 21, 2002.

19. See Daniel Mitchell, "OECD's perpetual tax grab," *Washington Times,* December 7, 2000; Walter Williams, "Global tax thuggery of OECD," *Washington Times,* December 29, 2000. The proposals are a clear recognition that Europe's high-tax, cradle-to-grave social welfare system is not "sustainable" without such an agreement. For a fascinating examination of the ways wealthy tax-exempt foundations fund environmental activism and lobby governments on issues like fossil fuels and climate change, see Ron Arnold, "The Pew Charitable Trusts: Global Warming Power Nexus," *Foundation Watch,* May 2004, Capital Research Center, www.CapitalResearch.org (publications).

20. Stephen Castle, "EU sends strong warning to Bush over greenhouse gas emissions," *The Independent* (London), March 19, 2001.

21. James Glassman, "The conservation myth stars as the latest (sub)urban legend," JewishWorldReview.com, June 14, 2001, citing Chirac's speech in November 2000 at the United Nation's COP-6 climate change conference at The Hague. For a revealing discussion of the global warming horror movie, "The Day After Tomorrow," see Patrick J. Michaels, "Apolalypse Soon? No, but this movie (and Democrats) hope you'll think so," *Washington Post,* May 16, 2004, http://www.washingtonpost.com/wp-dyn/articles/A28338-2004May14.html. As Micheals observes, the movie is "full of high-tech distortion" and its producers "live in a reality-free environment." The only way to trigger a new ice age caused by a "failure" of the Gulf Stream, notes Carl Wunsch, the world's leading authority on oceanic currents, "is either to turn off the earth's wind system, or stop the earth's rotation, or both." *See also* Paul Driessen, "The Day After the Day After Tomorrow," discussing the politics of global warming horror movies and other nightmarish scenarios, http://www.techcentralstation.com/042204D.html

9

Greenwashing for Greenbacks

Everybody is green these days – and rightly so. Virtually all of us
have become more concerned about wildlife and environmental
quality, more intent on reducing waste and pollution, more willing to
make the sustained investments in worthwhile projects and regulatory
programs that only wealthy nations can afford.

For some industries, being green is relatively easy. It's
toughest for companies engaged in manufacturing and the
"extractive industries" – the business of finding, harvesting and
extracting the energy and raw materials we need to enjoy the things
we have come to see as our birthright.

Every project should be conducted according to high
environmental standards. However, to condemn the extractive
industries or modern technology is misguided, at best. Indeed, even
the most ardent vegan or Earth Liberationist enjoys and benefits
from technology and what comes out of holes in the ground. Every
time they get dressed, drive a car or ride a bike, turn on a light or
computer, eat an apple, paint a house, turn the faucet to get fresh
water, play a CD, take an aspirin or get a vaccination, plant a tree,
or engage in any other mundane activity – they personally benefit
from resource extraction and the creative genius that has created
our modern world.

Virtually all extractive and manufacturing companies have improved the ways they produce, process and utilize raw materials. But some go the extra mile to be perceived by journalists, voters and eco-activists as being especially green. They engage continually in what the Concise Oxford English Dictionary defines as greenwashing: "disinformation disseminated by an organization so as to present an environmentally responsible public image."

Greenwashing perfectly describes BP's "Beyond Petroleum" ads and other public pronouncements that proclaim the company is much greener than its competitors: "Solar, natural gas, hydrogen, wind. And oh yes, oil. It's a start."

A minuscule start, perhaps, but enough to get the masters of spin and advertising hyperbole rolling along in a $100-million-a-year, self-congratulatory ad campaign.

> • Not long after spending $91 billion over two years to merge with Amoco and Arco, BP managed to scrape together $200 million for a 6-year solar program that included installing solar panels on 200 of its 17,000 service stations. That works out to 99.8 percent on oil, 0.2 percent on solar and solar panels on 1 percent of its stations.[1]
>
> • Its total 6-year solar investment is a mere 1.3 percent of what it plans to spend drilling for oil and gas in the Gulf of Mexico alone, over the next 15 years – and a minuscule 0.1 percent of the $27 billion it is spending to acquire and explore new oil prospects in Russia and other areas around the world.[2]
>
> • Its average annual $33 million solar investment equals a stunning 0.4 percent of its $8.5 billion 2001 petroleum expenditure … 0.02 percent of its 2002 net worth … or a third of what it spent each year on its "Beyond Petroleum" campaign.[3]

"If BP executives were completely honest about it," says the *Washington Times*, "they'd have to admit the company spends far more in a single year burnishing its environmental image than it has invested in solar power in the last six years."[4] And shareholder activist group SANE BP says the company spent more on its new eco-friendly helios logo than it did on renewable energy during all of 2000.[5]

"Beyond Petroleum," indeed. That's the epitome of greenwashing. Indeed, BP's renewable energy and "Great Beyondo" campaigns might be an excellent topic for a future segment of the Penn and Teller comedy team's Showtime original program, "Bullshit!"

But environmentalists still give BP relatively high marks, and an A for effort – even as they excoriate ExxonMobil as an eco-Darth Vader. And yet, ExxonMobil spent over $500 million on renewable energy R&D two decades ago (over $1 billion in 2002 dollars), before abandoning the effort as too fraught with scientific and economic uncertainty, and refocusing on fossil fuels.[6] The company still invests heavily in fuel cell technology, energy efficiency, and reducing carbon dioxide and other GHG emissions – for which it gets nothing but grief from the CSR and socially responsible investing crowd.

Meanwhile, ChevronTexaco's renewable energy division focuses on fuel cells, improved batteries (via a joint venture with Ovonics), hydrogen, wind and solar. But the company gets about as much green ink and acclaim for these environmental investments as does ExxonMobil.

Shell Oil Company also operates "a fledgling wind-power business" and, having purchased Siemen's solar photovoltaic operations, is now the fourth-largest solar-energy business in the world. The company also emphasizes biomass – burning wood in power plants to generate electricity. It is planning to invest $500 million to $1 billion in renewables over the next five years (and a like amount in oil shale), and believes there is "a chance" that renewable energy could become a profitable business over the next several decades.[7]

Shell's good public relations return on these image-building efforts is considerably higher than ExxonMobil's or Chevron-Texaco's. So is BP's. Maybe it pays to be so deeply involved in the World Business Council for Sustainable Development, and participate in SustainAbility's annual assessment of the "most socially responsible" companies.[8]

In contrast to its self-congratulatory "beyond" ads, BP is far more reticent when the conversation turns to drilling in Alaska's Arctic National Wildlife Refuge (ANWR). Yet, BP is the biggest operator on the North Slope, with huge lease holdings, and would certainly consider producing oil in the refuge if given the chance, admits John Mogford, BP vice president for renewable and alternative energy.[9]

How could the company responsibly take any other position? Government geologists estimate that ANWR could hold 6-16 billion barrels of recoverable oil. That's 11-30 years' of imports from Saudi Arabia. Turned into gasoline, it would power California's cars, trucks and Hollywood limousines for 18-50 years. And that's with old technology. Modern, constantly evolving exploration, drilling and production techniques could double this production, and keep the nearby Prudhoe Bay oil fields pumping another decade or more.

What drilling opponents likewise refuse to acknowledge is that every gallon we don't produce in the US is a gallon we have to import – often from countries that support terrorism. It's a gallon in hard-won energy conservation and renewable energy efforts wasted.

ANWR's oil would be produced from widely scattered sites totaling less than 2,000 acres. That's one-twentieth of Washington, DC, or 20 of the buildings Boeing uses to manufacture its 747 jets – in a refuge the size of South Carolina, in a state that has more designated wilderness than the combined acreage of Pennsylvania, New Jersey, Maryland and West Virginia.[10] Drilling would be done in the winter, when temperatures hover around minus 30 degrees Fahrenheit (-34 Celsius) and there is virtually no wildlife to be found – using ice airstrips, roads and platforms that melt when spring arrives.[11]

In the summer, caribou return, along with fox, birds, and vast swarms of vicious flies and mosquitoes. Even if drilling takes place, the caribou would do just what they have for 25 years in Prudhoe Bay: eat, hang out and make babies. That's why Prudhoe's caribou have increased from 5,000 in 1974 to 32,000 last year.

The Eskimos who live in ANWR know all this. Having seen their trapping and whaling activities curtailed by environmentalist pressure, they also know oil development may be their last chance to escape the poverty that has forced them to live in ramshackle homes, use five-gallon buckets for bathroom sanitation, and endure high rates of hepatitis and other diseases. As Kaktovik Inupiat Corporation president Fenton Rexford notes, the Eskimos are tired of living like this. Not surprisingly, they support ANWR oil development by an 8:1 margin.

The Gwich'in Indians, who oppose drilling, live 140 miles away and seem to have no problems with drilling on their own lands. They leased nearly every acre they own back in the 1980s and didn't even include provisions to protect caribou. Sadly, they didn't find any oil. Now they're planning to drill and build a pipeline along the caribou migratory route in Canada, even as they continue to take large sums of money from environmental groups for opposing oil drilling on Eskimo land.

But mentioning these facts (especially in the midst of its ad campaign) could tarnish BP's greener-than-our-competitors image. So the company quietly pulled out of the ANWR debate and the pro-drilling trade association, Arctic Power – while keeping its onshore Alaska drilling options open and building an artificial drilling island in the Beaufort Sea off the Prudhoe Bay coast.

Meanwhile, BP was handed a maximum criminal penalty of $500,000 by a US District Court in 2000, for failing to report the illegal disposal of hazardous waste on Alaska's North Slope. The company was also ordered to pay $15 million over the next five years to "establish a nationwide environmental management system designed to prevent future violations" – in addition to the $6.5 million that it agreed to pay in civil penalties.[12]

In January 2001, BP was assessed a $10 million penalty and agreed to spend $500 million modernizing its pollution-control equipment, for violating federal clean-air laws at eight US refineries. It also faces charges for alleged safety violations that led to one death, a seriously burned worker and a dozen other injuries at its Prudhoe Bay facilities in 2002 alone.[13]

On the other hand, to underscore how green it is, BP is clearly at the forefront of efforts to secure ratification of the Kyoto Protocol on global climate change. It may be that Sir John Browne sincerely believes the global warming theorists and computer models are right – even in the absence of any satellite or other empirical evidence to corroborate them. However, as discussed previously, one can justifiably suspect other motives.

The entire climate change process strikes many as a monumental exercise in make-believe problems with make-believe solutions – much as in the case of a Hollywood horror movie blockbuster (with billions of dollars in potential royalties for the producers and script writers).[14]

And yet, BP gets tremendous mileage out of "being green" for its support of the Kyoto Protocol and for actions it has taken to reduce greenhouse gases and prevent catastrophic global warming. Indeed, BP loves to be "green." As in the color of greenwashing – and the color of money.

Clearly, what is needed here is a healthy dose of skepticism – something like the kind Greenpeace employed in 1999 when it presented Sir John Browne with an Academy Award for giving the "Best Impression of an Environmentalist."

Of course, BP is hardly alone in touting its questionable environmental credentials.

CNN founder Ted Turner is a greenwasher *non pareil.* He sponsors elite bison hunts at $10,500 per hunter ... erected "killer fences" that snare and strangle migrating wildlife ... cuts timber ... drills for natural gas ... and even bulldozed a hilltop to give himself a better view of a mountain range – all on his Montana ranch. The ranch is part of his 1.8 million acres in US real estate holdings (Delaware is only 1.3 million acres) and part of an empire that includes an Argentina ranch that Turner regularly flies to in his private jet. The billionaire also received more than $217,000 in American taxpayer agricultural subsidies between 1996 and 2000.[15]

Most corporate tycoons would be pilloried and hauled into court by environmental groups for such actions. They might even receive midnight visits from Earth and Animal Liberation Front eco-terrorists. But Turner gets a free pass. Greens don't even ask him to conduct an "energy audit," to determine how many Btus he consumes in a year, for his sprawling ranches, SUVs and other vehicles, private jets, fancy entertaining, pricey hotel accommodations, heating and air conditioning for his mansions and servants quarters, and the other accoutrements of his celebrity lifestyle.

(Come to think of it, the greens never ask these embarrassing questions of Robert Redford, Barbra Streisand, Leonardo DiCaprio, Ted Kennedy or other energy scolds, either. Leo flew from LA to DC, then was chauffeured in a stretch limo to give an impassioned "save the planet" speech to Earth Day 2000 multitudes. Celebs took so many limos and SUVs to EarthFair 2000 and the 2002 Academy Awards that its VIP parking lot was filled to capacity with gas-guzzlers – for anti-car-choice harridans like Friends of the Earth president Jaynie Chase and husband Chevy, who never tire of hectoring lesser Americans about the virtues of energy conservation.[16] Ditto for House Democratic Leader Dick Gephardt, who took his SUV to an Exxon station to denounce President Bush for including "only" 42 conservation measures in the Administration's 2001 energy bill.)

One can't help but conclude that Mr. Turner gets a free pass from green activists because he donates millions to environmental causes, enabling radicals to shut down other people's cattle ranches, stop medical experiments and other people's "cruelty" to animals, close vast acreage of public and other people's land to timber cutting and oil drilling, lobby against SUVs and other "extravagant" fuel consumption by ordinary Americans, and prevent global warming, caused by other people's excessive jet travel and SUV use. Ditto for the Hollywood glitterati.

ExxonMobil, on the other hand, is (properly) viewed as the antithesis of greenwashing. In fact, it is regularly excoriated by self-styled environmentalists for its unflinching views on climate change and oil drilling, and its adamant refusal to bow to radical green demands.

They point out that the company refuses to invest any more money in renewable energy projects, and persuaded the vast majority of its shareholders to vote against a pro-renewable-energy resolution at its May 2002 annual meeting. However, while thumbing its nose at environmental activists, the company has worked without fanfare on energy conservation, pollution reduction, artificial reef and other initiatives.

- It claims its refineries and chemical plants reduced greenhouse gas emissions by over 35 percent (200 million metric tons) during the past 25 years, and achieved similar improvements in energy efficiency in those facilities over the same period.
- ExxonMobil has also expanded co-generation at its refineries and chemical plants, using "waste" heat to generate electricity and steam for other uses. In conjunction with Toyota and General Motors, it is researching fuel cells to develop technologies that lower carbon emissions and increase fuel efficiency.[17]

• In late 2002, the company joined General Electric, Schlumberger and European energy distributor EOn, to sponsor a 10-year, $225 million dollar a year research project by Stanford University. The program will assess which alternative energy technologies offer the greatest promise, how today's major suppliers of energy can become even cleaner, and how these technological advances could obviate the need for drastic reductions in US energy use, to address the concerns some have about global warming.[18]

• It also undertook a major effort to preserve rare tigers and their Asian habitats. The Save the Tiger campaign was undoubtedly as much an effort to save its marketing symbol ("Put a tiger in your tank"), as it was a wildlife conservation program. But plaudits were rare, until November 2002, when the World Wildlife Fund lauded the campaign, saying ExxonMobil's efforts were "probably the most significant corporate contribution to endangered species conservation ever."[19]

ChevronTexaco has undertaken similar energy efficiency and pollution reduction projects, and is also working on fuel cells, improved batteries, and hydrogen, wind and solar programs. The Sun Company has carried out a major alternative fuel automotive program for many years.

Both Ford Motor Company and General Motors recently decided to abandon their electric car programs – Ford after spending more than $100 million, GM after exhausting over $1 billion of shareholders' capital. Both decisions underscore the dangers of allowing environmental politics – rather than sound business and economic sense – to determine investment decisions.[20]

Many of these efforts are certainly comparable to BP's. And yet, more often than not, it is BP that pats itself on the back, runs expensive print and television ads, actively courts acclamation for its programs, and gets singled out by friendly journalists and environmentalists as the epitome of social responsibility and planetary concern.

Of course, not all environmentalists are persuaded. Climate activist Kenny Bruno charges that steps taken by any oil company – including BP – to reduce its own GHG emissions are "symbolic" and irrelevant, because the companies' impact on hypothetical global warming is primarily due to the emissions by consumers using their petroleum products.

"If we measure those emissions," he claims, "Shell alone accounts for more carbon dioxide than most countries in the world." Thus, on a symbolic level, Shell and BP may have broken with unrepentant ExxonMobil and embraced the Kyoto Protocol. But on a practical level, they are just as bad as their "hard-line counterpart," because what they offer is mostly "sophisticated, soothing rhetoric," and they are still drilling for oil and gas "anywhere and everywhere."[21]

The lesson should be plain for all to see. Greenwashing is dishonest, quixotic – and political spin in its purest form. It is especially so for companies whose core business involves extracting raw materials or manufacturing automobiles, fuels or other essential products. Most of us see these activities as causing short term, repairable ecological damage to meet people's needs. Radical greens, however, view them as "eviscerating" and "raping" Mother Earth, "depleting finite resources," and "spewing toxic chemicals into fragile ecosystems," leading us further from their goal of "perfect balance with Nature, as epitomized by primitive Amazonians."

Greenwashing is also a depressing commentary on what Greenpeace co-founder-turned-arch-critic Patrick Moore observes has increasingly happened to a movement he helped launch. As the environmental movement "gained power, it succumbed to political and social activists who learned to use environmental rhetoric to cloak agendas that have little to do with ecology. Our original vision of Spaceship Earth and one human family was stolen and transformed into a virulent attack on corporations, technology, trade and science."[22]

The environmentalists certainly began with legitimate grievances about serious threats to the natural world. But over the years, the movement's more radical elements have become more dominant, more intolerant in their views, more insatiable in their demands, and more disingenuous in their claims about hypothetical risks from chemicals, pesticides, fossil fuels, biotechnology and other manifestations of modern society.

In their constant litany of doom and gloom, they have refused to acknowledge what, by any rational standards, are major improvements in air and water quality, tremendous reductions in the use of fuels and raw materials per unit of economic output, and significant declines in the rate of human population growth. Even a recent study, by Conservation International – demonstrating that nearly one-half of the Earth's surface remains an untouched wilderness, and tropical rainforests remain largely intact – generated cries of disbelief and outrage by more radical groups.[23]

Ideological environmentalists have also become callously indifferent to the suffering that their policies are causing for hundreds of millions of people who face daily struggles merely to feed their families and stay alive.

Perhaps even worse, every attempt to appease these organizations is doomed to failure. They can never be satisfied, and every attempt at greenwashing plays further into their hands – further enriching and empowering their organizations, and making true progress and better lives for the most miserable inhabitants of our planet even more difficult.

It is yet another reason why responsible companies, politicians and citizens must begin to:

• Challenge these radical groups and their greenwashing corporate and investor accomplices;
• Ensure that the environmental alarmist movement does not remain the only multinational industry that is not governed by basic rules for ethics, false and deceptive advertising, transparency, disclosure and accountability – rules the movement has long demanded of for-profit corporations; and
• Question the extent to which ideological environmentalists represent the public interest. Question their assertions, expertise, standing, legitimacy and agenda. Question their definitions of corporate social responsibility, sustainable development and the precautionary principle.
• Learn more about the vital roles that biotechnology, pesticides, energy, trade, economic development and safe water play in ensuring healthy, prosperous nations that provide hope, better lives and improved environmental quality for their people.

Most importantly, they need to listen more to the views of Third World community leaders, health care workers, and local citizens like John Aluma, Fifi Kobusingye, Leon Louw, Barun Mitra, Jim Muhwezi, Gordon Mwesigye, James Shikwati, Richard Tren, Shalini Wadhwa and Florence Wambugu. They need to let these people's experiences, aspirations and pleas guide them through the thickets of conflicting claims and give them the moral courage to confront ideological extremists who seek to impose their agendas on the destitute people of the developing world.

Chapter Nine Footnotes

1. Cait Murphy, "Is BP Beyond Petroleum? Hardly," *Fortune*, September 30, 2002.
2. *Ibid.*
3. *Ibid.*; "The climate greenwash vanguard: Shell and BP Amoco," Corporate Europe Observatory Issue Briefing (undated); Darcy Frey, "How green is BP?" *New York Times Magazine*, December 8, 2002.
4. "Currying favor with the green lobby," editorial, *Washington Times*, October 12, 2002; "BP: Oil Giant Spends Big to Promote Green Image," *Greenwire*, December 6, 2000.
5. Kenny Bruno, "A convenient confusion," *New Internationalist 335*, June 2001. SANE BP is made up of Greenpeace, the US Public Interest Research Group (USPIRG), and "socially responsible" investors in the United States and Britain, at times joined by Trillium Asset Management Corporation.
6. Heesun Wee, "Can oil giants and green energy mix?" *Business Week Online*, September 25, 2002.
7. Steve Raabe, "Shell exec: Patience may pay off for oil shale, renewables," *Denver Post*, May 13, 2002.
8. See page 9 and Chapter One Footnotes, note 14. See also Chapter 10.
9. Heesun Wee, "Can oil giants and green energy mix?" *Business Week Online*, September 25, 2002; "Currying favor with the green lobby," editorial, *Washington Times,* October 12, 2002.
10. Statutorily designated wilderness areas are completely closed to energy and mineral exploration, timber cutting (even to control insect infestations and forest fires), vehicles (including bicycles and wheel chairs), buildings of any kind, and permanent trails. Many wilderness users do not even want to see or hear vehicles or other uses from within the designated areas, meaning that "buffer zones" are often created around wilderness areas.
11. Paul Driessen, "Help for California's energy crisis," *Washington Times*, February 8, 2001; "California's Crisis Means ANWR Should Be Opened," *Capitalism Magazine*, June 5, 2001.
12. *Environment News Service*, February 2, 2000.
13. Andrew Gumbel and Marie Woolf, "Beyond petroleum, or beyond the pale? BP left out in the cold," *Independent News* (UK), January 23, 2003.
14. See for example, James M. Taylor, "Still no consensus on global warming science," *Environment & Climate News*, January 2003; Paul Driessen, "Halloween 13: Global warming horror movies," Still Waiting for Greenhouse website, http://www.vision.net.au/~daly/horror.htm

15. Audrey Hudson, "Greens cut Turner a break," *Washington Times,* January 20, 2002. The most common environmental group nickname for Ted Turner is "Daddy Greenbucks," according to Barry Clausen, private investigator and author of *Burning Rage.*
16. Energy scold "Malibu Babs" Streisand sued a photographer for posting pictures of the diva's home on the Internet. "What really must bother Streisand," wrote Michelle Malkin, "is that anyone can now click on the Internet photos to see her six environmentally incorrect chimneys and chlorine-guzzling swimming pool. It's what the photos of Streisand's mansion don't show – no windmill-powered generators, no electric cars, no 'Small is Beautiful' lawn ornaments, no hemp curtains in the windows of her eight bedrooms and 11 bathrooms, no Scaasi evening gowns hanging outside to dry on clotheslines that should be strung between her precious parasols – that expose the truth of her eco-hypocrisy best." Michelle Malkin, "Malibu Babs: Snapshots of an eco-hypocrite," townhall.com, June 4, 2003.
17. See www.ExxonMobil.com/corporate – Actions and Results – Safeguarding Our Environment; "Cogeneration and climate," *The Lamp,* Fall 2001; Thomas Torget, "Corporate citizenship in a changing world: New publication examines ExxonMobil's business principles and commitments," *The Lamp,* Fall 2002.
18. See Paul Driessen, "Global warming review could prevent EU gaffe," Columbia (MO) *Tribune,* November 26, 2002.
19. Marc Morano, "Greens praise ExxonMobil for efforts to save tiger," CNSNews.com, November 22, 2002. ExxonMobil has invested $10.3 million in 13 habitats since the fund's inception in 1995, and recruited martial arts action star Jackie Chan and other celebrities to publicize the cause.
20. See "California retreat on emissions upsets 'car of the future' buyers," *Washington Times,* April, 9, 2003. The decision reflects consumer rejection of expensive cars with a range of less than 100 miles on a single charge.
21. Kenny Bruno, "A convenient confusion," *New Internationalist 335,* June 2001.
22. Nick Nichols, *Rules for Corporate Warriors: How to fight and survive attack group shakedowns,* Bellevue, WA: Free Enterprise Press (2001), Introduction by Patrick Moore.
23. See Marc Morano, "Study's Authors 'Surprised' to Find Nearly Half of Earth's Wilderness Intact," CNSNews.com, December 6, 2002; and "Global Analysis Finds Nearly Half The Earth Is Still Wilderness," press release from Conservation International, December 4, 2002.

Eco-Imperialism

10

Investor Fraud

Do some investment advisory firms use misleading, even fraudulent, tactics to denigrate certain companies and attract investors to competitor companies favored by the advisors? Do their promises and projections about future earnings reflect dubious energy and environmental claims? Do cozy relationships among foundations, corporations, activists, and "socially responsible" investor groups and stock analysts further this strategy?

Unfortunately, the disturbing answer appears to be yes.

Investors lost billions in 2002, when the deceitful practices of Enron, Global Crossing, WorldCom, Tyco, Arthur Anderson and other companies became public, and their financial house of cards came crashing down.

Fortune, Business Week, the *Washington Post* and *New York Times*, activists, citizens and politicians alike made impassioned pleas for prosecutions, new laws and tougher penalties. These actions, they said, were needed to curb widespread patterns of cooking the books, shading the truth, misleading statements and other distortions of facts and accounting figures, breaches of trust, abuses of power, unfair enrichment and even outright fraud.

Arrests followed, corporate crooks were prosecuted, and Congress enacted the Sarbanes-Oxley "corporate reform law." In the process, many legislators failed to recognize that part of the problem was the regulators' past failure to investigate, regulate and enforce existing laws. They also assumed the nature and scope of the problem was worse than it actually was, and wound up criminalizing even inadvertent or minor accounting errors, imperfect research, estimation errors and write-downs.[1]

Despite extensive attention to this corporate misfeasance and malfeasance, however, some dubious practices escaped notice, and continue today. Two Roman proverbs are particularly relevant to this continuing deception. *Caveat emptor*: "Let the buyer beware" – not only of corporate practices, but of what is being pedaled as sound or "ethical" investments by politically active organizations. *Qui custodiet ipses custodies?* "Who will guard the guards" who claim to be watchdogs for the public interest?

The hard reality is that some companies, investment advisors, foundations and activist groups still have not gotten the message. Sometimes, it's because they wear three hats at one time, creating real or potential conflicts of interest.

> • They are corporations – even huge multinationals – some for-profit, others not-for-profit.
> • They may serve as financial advisors, urging consumers and investors to put their money into companies that they assert are ethical, green or socially responsible, and pull their money out of companies they portray as environmental or human rights Darth Vaders.
> • They may also be social activists, vigorously promoting certain energy, economic and environmental agendas that reflect their ideologies and help fill their own coffers, often with little regard for the best interests of people, especially the world's poor.

Perhaps now is the time to ensure that our old, new and rediscovered principles and standards are applied across the board. They must govern not just companies, but also activist NGOs, analysts, advisors and foundations that at times engage in deceptive, even Enronesque practices, to further their political, ideological and financial goals.

The advice offered so freely for corporate reform in 2002 might be a good starting point for further house cleaning, to inspire government oversight and better enforcement of ethical principles for activist nonprofit organizations. Here is a sampling of that advice.

• Companies should require: codes of ethics for their boards of directors, annual (public) performance evaluations of directors, and directors who are truly outsiders – independent from the company, with no ties to the CEO, and no dependence on the company for special benefits or their livelihoods.[2]

• Companies need to replace CEOs who fail at moral leadership, accountants who engage in "borderline accounting," and directors who fail to direct, have vested interests in maintaining systems that are beneficial to them, are "asleep at the wheel," or don't want to "rock the boat."[3]

• Corporations should also strive to create cultures that "encourage and reward integrity as much as entrepreneurship" and hire executives who are "not only exemplary managers but also the moral compass for the company." To establish a system of checks and balances that insures against companies "crossing the ethical divide," they should provide the CEO with a "roomful of skeptics" and should actively encourage dissent.[4]

• Companies must no longer employ the "arrogant, closed-culture" approach. They cannot presume that they know what is best "not only for the organizations, but for affected constituents." Nor can they assume they are "immune from responsibility for their actions [because they are] too large, or too powerful, or too vital to a community to worry about accountability."[5]

• Companies should be required to state income, expenditures and profits "in a way that is more meaningful and less subject to manipulation." Even if companies "want to tout random, unaudited, watch-me-pull-a-rabbit-out-of-my-hat figures in their press releases," investors should "immediately be able to compare these figures with full financial statements prepared in accordance with Generally Accepted Accounting Principles."[6]

• Accountants and auditors should not be permitted to merely "sign off on clients' financial statements. They should also have to grade the quality of their earnings."[7] Because they are in "a unique position to judge how dependent the financial statements are on assumptions that could prove faulty," accountants and auditors also need to exercise much more skepticism and not conduct merely "cursory reviews."[8]

• To ensure research with integrity and avoid conflicts of interest, analysts must disclose any actual and apparent conflicts of interest. They must go beyond putting out glowing recommendations that are "long on concepts and potentials, but short on facts and figures." They should not be allowed to participate in investment-banking deals, or make recommendations on buying stocks, while simultaneously selling their advice to the companies whose stocks they cover.[9]

• And finally, from shareholder activist Robert Monks: Our legal system and companies should empower institutional owners to hold corporate managers accountable for their actions and the consequences thereof (especially in the social, environmental and human rights arenas), to ensure that corporate interests truly reflect "the goals of society as a whole."[10]

Curing corporate malfeasance, accounting fraud and conflicted advice can also be summed up in Charles Schwab's three core principles.

Transparency – conducting business and making decisions "in the light of day," with integrity, honesty and input from investors, consumers, the institutions that serve them, and the "stakeholders" that are most affected by them.

Disclosure – giving investors and the general public a clear picture of the biases and conflicts built into the advice they receive, and providing easy access to that information, so that they can make informed choices.

Accountability – at the senior-most executive levels, for actions and their consequences, under codes of conduct that require the CEO and chief compliance officer to certify that the proper controls are in place.[11]

But will these basic principles now be applied in other arenas, where passivity and a too-narrow focus have led to numerous abuses that continue to cry out for reform?

America has long prided itself on having a single legal system that applies equally to all citizens, does not permit selected groups to live by different standards, and imposes the same duties and penalties on all. But this system of equal justice for all has lost its bearings.

In this critically important era – when for-profit and not-for-profit corporations, activist groups, investment advisory firms, institutional investor funds and major foundations all exert enormous influence on our economy, public policies and the performance of individual companies – our system allows these selected groups to play by very different rules.

Not only are these activists exempt from false advertising, transparency, financial disclosure and accountability rules. But recent legislative and regulatory reforms apply primarily or only to the for-profit corporate sector, despite widespread patterns of abuse within these exempt nonprofit sectors.

Having spent much of 2002 addressing corporate fraud, our watchdog groups, journalists, legislators, regulators and courts must now devote their attention to correcting abuses that have become prevalent in these other sectors. The principles noted above would provide excellent guidelines for long overdue reforms.

Eldridge Cleaver used to say, "If you're not part of the solution, you're part of the problem." Today, many activist and institutional investor groups have clearly become part of the problem.

Pension and mutual funds today own nearly $8 trillion in market share! A mere 75 mutual funds, pensions and other institutional shareholders control $6.3 trillion worth of stock – some 44 percent of the total stock market. In fact, pension funds are now the largest owners of US companies, and the California Public Employees Retirement System (CalPERS) is the most influential institutional investor of all.[12]

Robert A.G. Monks, the oft-quoted shareholder activist, says pension fund investors "want to retire into a clean, civil and safe world." Monks' plan is to "empower institutional owners to hold corporate managers accountable for their actions" and "align corporate interests with the goals of society as a whole." This, he says, will compel CEOs to factor the social and environmental concerns of their long-term stakeholders into all their decisions, and bring corporate and government programs in line with the agendas he and his activist investors have charted.[13]

To move this process along, Monks advises, energizes and even funds shareholder campaigns that help "persuade" CEOs to adopt his social and environmental platforms. Most of these campaigns are led by liberal church groups, labor unions, "socially conscious" mutual funds, public sector pension funds like CalPERS, radical activist groups like Greenpeace and Campaign ExxonMobil, and large foundations (that often set the agendas for activist groups they support).

Their passion for The Cause is revealed in comments that Father Michael Crosby, director of the Interfaith Center on Corporate Responsibility, made to Dr. Ray Bohlin, executive director of Probe Ministries, after Dr. Bohlin opposed a shareholder resolution that Father Crosby had introduced at the 2002 ExxonMobil annual meeting.

"You disrespected the Gospel," Father Crosby told him, by using Christian references to oppose the resolution, and "must have been duped into saying those things."[14]

At the international level, environmental activists have now become an $8-billion-a-year industry. For the most part, it is subject to none of the laws that govern for-profit corporations on matters of transparency, disclosure, false advertising and accountability.[15]

But what happens when the concerns and proposed solutions of these activists and institutional investors result in additional problems for the poorest people on the planet – those who have not yet shared the dreams and successes of the developed world? What if creating a "clean, civil and safe world" for Monks' retirees results in a less clean, civil and safe world for people in Africa, Asia and Latin America?

What if, for instance, CalPERS' "socially conscious" agenda includes opposition to energy and economic development, pesticide use, biotechnology, trade, menial jobs and other programs that people half a planet away desperately want and critically need? Whose agenda then determines what are to be "the goals of society as a whole"? Equally important, who has given these activists the moral or legal authority to impose their goals – and the consequences thereof, intended and otherwise – on people who do not agree with the goals, must live with the consequences and had no role in making the decisions?

Who will hold Robert Monks, the institutional investors, and the various church, environmental and other activists "accountable for *their* actions"? What is to be *their* "moral compass," provide them a system of checks and balances, and ensure that a healthy measure of skepticism and dissent presides when they pressure corporations to do their bidding?

How can our legal and political systems ensure that these activists do not remain an "arrogant, closed-culture" that "knows what's best" for affected constituents and believes it is "immune from responsibility because it is too vital to the community" to be hauled onto the carpet?

How do we ensure that activist groups don't tout phony, unaudited income and spending figures, bogus scientific and statistical data, and other suspect claims? How can we guarantee that sympathetic or merely gullible regulators, judges and journalists do not simply sign off on these statements, ignore glaring conflicts of interest, or allow activists, investment analysts and institutional investors to collaborate on agendas that ill serve investors, voters and the poor?

Monks and his activist allies have spent years crusading for the principles that have now been imposed on (or voluntarily adopted by) for-profit corporations. If the principles are to mean anything as fundamental arbiters of ethical behavior, they should certainly apply with equal force and effect to the crusaders themselves.

Institutional Shareholder Services was founded by Robert Monks to research companies, offer investment advice to pension funds and other institutional investors, and recommend shareholder resolutions on renewable energy and gay rights. ISS has 300 employees, 750 institutional clients and "real clout," and Monks is a "key behind-the-scenes advisor" to the trustees of CalPERS and other huge institutional investor groups. He's also written books and articles on "ethical investing" and on corporate power, social responsibility and accountability.[16]

To track the supposed "relationship between Corporate Social Responsibility and shareholder value," he developed a "simulation program" called Brightline. This program was used by former Chase Investment Bank analyst Mark Mansley to assess the "reputational damage and litigation risks that ExxonMobil could face if it did not make changes" advocated by Monks and other "ethical investment" activists.[17]

Monks helped underwrite the Mansley report, *Risking Shareholder Value? ExxonMobil and Climate Change.* Issued under the auspices of Claros Consulting in London, the report became a centerpiece for a years-long shareholder campaign against ExxonMobil. Monks also "gave money and advice" to the coalition of church groups and environmentalists who ran "Campaign ExxonMobil."[18]

But despite these obvious and intricate relationships with radical activists, ISS still gets a free pass from the media. Even the *Wall Street Journal* simply has called it "an adviser to pension and mutual fund managers" and uncritically reported its endorsement of shareholder resolutions "by investor activists" to compel companies like American Electric Power "to disclose how its status as a major emitter could cost the company big money" because of supposed impacts on global climate.[19]

The "solution" proposed by activists – closing coal-fired power plants and shifting to *natural* gas – ignores the lack of scientific evidence to support catastrophic global warming theories. It also glosses over fact that the same activist groups also oppose drilling for natural gas almost anywhere in the United States, including public lands in western states, Alaska and off the coasts.

CalPERS, the California Public Employees Retirement System, has long been a leader of the CSR movement. Unfortunately, it has not been a leader among pension funds for retirees whose future depends on sound investments.

As a *Wall Street Journal* editorial noted, the fund "has begun to tailor more of its investment calls to an ideological agenda. CalPERS' fiduciary duty is to its 1.3 million public employees and their families, who expect a solid return on their money." The fund "claims to keep a watch over business, but someone is going to have to keep a more careful eye on CalPERS."[20]

In the late 1990s, it made significant investments in "ethical" companies like Enron, WorldCom and BP – and economic powerhouses like Argentina – which somehow met CalPERS' slippery criteria for "socially responsible investing." In early 2002, it withdrew its investment from countries like Malaysia, because NGOs and its union trustees criticized the countries' labor standards.

Malaysia's wages had doubled in the 1990s, unemployment was below 3 percent, and nearly a third of its workforce was foreign guest workers, who got jobs because of investment in Malaysia. But none of that seemed to matter, especially since a number of Malaysian companies compete with California electronics companies and discourage unionizing.

The pension fund lost $20 billion during the first two years of this century. As a result, many of its investors may face a less rosy retirement. One could reasonably conclude that CalPERS' fiduciary duty to its investors apparently has given way to an assumed duty to activist groups. Its actions betrayed the trust of these investors every bit as much as did the actions of corporate and Wall Street bigwigs who are now being prosecuted by the State of New York and Securities and Exchange Commission.

Claros Consulting is a UK-based firm that provides "expert information and advice on socially responsible investment (SRI) for institutional investors." It publishes an online Guide to Socially Responsible Investment for Pension Funds, "covering what it is, how to develop an SRI policy, the legal position, the various issues and approaches."[21]

Once the polite euphemisms are stripped away, however, what Claros and its allies actually operate is what some might call a sophisticated "protection racket" and shakedown operation. While allied groups engage in hijinks like those popularized by Greenpeace and Campaign ExxonMobil, Claros employs more modern weaponry – such as politicized financial analyses that are used in concert with shareholder resolutions and the hardcore radicals' more theatrical tactics.

One of the more highly sophisticated examples is Mark Mansley's shareholder value "analysis," which was sponsored by

Campaign ExxonMobil, Robert Monks and the Coalition for Environmentally Responsible Economies (CERES), to promote various shareholder resolutions.

It claims ExxonMobil's market capitalization could fall by "as much as 10 percent (or about $20 billion)" because of the company's "refusal to take global warming seriously" or invest further in renewable energy technologies. It also asserts that ExxonMobil could lose up to $50 billion from damaged reputation alone, face a loss of insurability, and be subjected to mass tort liability lawsuits for damaging the earth's climate.

However, in a teleconference arranged by Claros to promote its report shortly before the May 2002 ExxonMobil annual meeting –

> • Monks relied on *ad hominem* attacks that accused ExxonMobil and other companies of being "dictators with vast power, who refuse to be accountable to what their owners require," and
> • Mansley admitted that much of his report was based – not on actual data and analysis – but rather on unproven assumptions about catastrophic global climate change, and on primitive computer models that claim to analyze the highly complex and dynamic US and global economies. His answer to one of the last questions was sprinkled with "I think" and "I am fairly sure," and concluded:
> • "The results are ... only an economic analysis. They are only going to be an approximation of the truth, but the results appear reasonable. They appear to reflect reality."[22]

However, "an approximation of the truth" and computer model results that "appear to reflect reality" hardly support the report's obdurate conclusions or justify attempts to coerce a company into adopting radical green policies on fossil fuels, renewable energy and climate change.

The report's conflicts of interest are blatant and obvious. There is little of substance to back up its criticisms, and its rampant guesswork make the "analysis" meaningless and subject to easy manipulation. In fact, its unaudited data and conclusions rely so heavily on rank conjecture about future energy, technology and climate scenarios that they violate Generally Accepted Accounting Principles and offer virtually nothing of substance to support the report's dire predictions, or give people reliable enough data to make informed investment decisions.

If the Claros report were correct, investors should already be giving the greener, more politically correct companies higher valuations in the stock market. That has not happened. In fact, "villainous" ExxonMobil has been among the energy industry's most consistently strong performers in recent years.

- It had sales of $213 billion in 2001 and netted $15 billion, making it the most profitable company in the United States. Annual total returns to ExxonMobil shareholders averaged 13 percent over the past five years, and the annual dividend payment increased in 2001 for the 19th consecutive year. (Profits were lower in 2002, as ExxonMobil suffered a significant profit decline in the third quarter 2002, as did Royal Dutch Shell.)
- ExxonMobil's price-earnings (P/E) ratio was 24.4 in Q3-2002, compared to 19.0 for Shell and 50.7 (!) for BP. ExxonMobil's $1.44 return on shareholder's equity was slightly below the Royal Dutch/Shell return of $1.47/$1.57, but well above BP's $0.78 return.
- J.P. Morgan said in March 2002 that ExxonMobil "deserves to trade at a premium valuation." Goldman Sachs agreed, adding that the company's "strong management team and impressive pool of employees allow investors to sleep well at night." The first quarter 2002 *Value Line Investment Survey* noted that ExxonMobil had the highest return on equity in the entire petroleum sector in 2001. And Peter Lynch's "Guru" profile gave it good marks in October 2002: a "100%" score and a "fast grower" rating.
- According to the 2002 Forbes Platinum 400 list of blue-chip companies based or operating in the United States, ExxonMobil had a 5-year average 14.0 percent return on capital (profitability), and a 10.4 percent return in 2002; its 2002 profit margin was 5.9 percent. By contrast, BP's 5-year average was 10.1 percent; its 2002 return a meager 5.7 percent; its profit margin only 2.9 percent in 2002.[23]

During 2002, chief executive Lord John Browne was forced
to lower BP's production estimates three times, resulting in a drop
of return on average capital to 11 percent for the year, compared
to 13.7 percent and 14.8 percent for archrivals ExxonMobil and
Royal Dutch/Shell, respectively. As a result, in an effort to lure
more investors, BP was persuaded to put the Petroleum back into
British Petroleum, in an effort to get Back to Profits.[24]

Thus, when Claros claims ExxonMobil's fossil fuel, climate
change and renewable energy strategies put it at a competitive
disadvantage, what it really means is that radical activists have
singled the company out for boycotts, protests and agenda-driven
shareholder resolutions.

When Claros says institutional investors are making climate
change a high priority in their investment decisions, it actually means
Claros, its allied groups and other green activists are lobbying them
to do so and intend to continue their high-pressure, protection-racket
tactics.

And when Monks, ISS, Claros, CERES, Innovest and
Campaign ExxonMobil engage in the "borderline accounting" and
shoddy analysis reflected in Mansley's report, what they are also doing
is promoting their own ideologies, vested interests and bottom lines.

Monks *et al.* will no doubt argue that these murky alliances,
secretive payment arrangements, questionable analyses, relentlessly
upbeat reports about favored companies, and routinely negative
reviews of politically incorrect companies are somehow different
from the actions of infamous Wall Street securities firms: Goldman
Sachs, Merrill Lynch, Morgan Stanley and Salomon Smith Barney,
to name but a few. Less self-interested observers will beg to disagree.

Under any reasonable definition and interpretation of the
law – particularly in the wake of Enron, WorldCom, Global Crossing
and the Sarbanes-Oxley corporate reform law – this smoke and
mirrors "analysis" and shakedown attempt is deceptive and
unethical. This and similar tactics should be investigated by
Congress, the Federal Trade Commission and the Securities and
Exchange Commission.

Campaign ExxonMobil is determined to compel ExxonMobil to
take a "responsible position on global warming" and make "serious
investments in solutions." Its tactics include street theater, letter
writing campaigns, shareholder resolutions, kangaroo court trials

to "convict" the company of human rights violations and "unrestrained corporate power," and thinly veiled threats of lawsuits and "direct action."[25]

But there's more here than meets the eye – and more than Campaign ExxonMobil wants people to see.

- Campaign members and advisers include the Committee in Solidarity with the People of Iraq, North Texas Islamic Association, UPROAR, Anarchist Black Cross, Industrial Workers of the World, Monkeywrench Collective, PressurePoint, Ruckus Society, NRDC, CERES, Ralph Nader's USPIRG and former members of the Black Panther Party.
- Campaign ExxonMobil is actually a front group for the Texas Fund for Energy and Environmental Education. TFEEE, in turn, gets its money from the Energy Foundation, a conglomerate of seven giant liberal foundations – the Rockefeller Foundation, Pew Charitable Trusts, John D. and Catherine T. MacArthur Foundation, Packard Foundation, Hewlett Foundation, McKnight Foundation and Joyce Mertz-Gilmore Foundation. These giants have combined assets of $21 billion, mostly in multinationals other than ExxonMobil.
- Campaign coordinator Chris Doran also works for Greenpeace and for another activist group appropriately called PressurePoint.
- PressurePoint gets its money from Downwinders at Risk, a virtually unfunded group that acts as a monetary conduit for the very leftish Samuel Rubin Foundation, which (like the TFEEE foundations) is heavily invested in multinational companies.
- Another major player in the anti-ExxonMobil effort is CorpWatch, which hides under the umbrella of the Tides Center, a secretive "donor-advised fund" that gets large sums from corporations, big-money foundations and other donors.

But figuring out these assorted front groups, shells, interconnections and money laundering schemes takes hours of painstaking research, because none of this information is readily available to the average investor or concerned citizen.

"The relationships between attack groups in this campaign are extremely complicated and difficult to trace," notes activist watchdog Ron Arnold. "There are shells within shells within shells. Assumed names are common. Ironically, the non-profit attack groups that scream loudest, demanding full disclosure from the for-profit sector, are themselves the most secretive and invisible to public scrutiny."[26]

Why all these secretive relationships and payments? Why don't these radical activists follow the laws, ethical guidelines, and precepts for honesty, transparency and social responsibility that they demand of for-profit corporations? How can any investor, regulator or journalist trust anything they say?

The Dow Jones Sustainability Index tracks the stock market performance of 300 global companies whose business practices have received a green seal of approval from an outfit called Sustainable Asset Management. Index promoters claim that there "does seem to be evidence that corporate sustainability can create shareholder value…. There is also evidence that investors can take advantage of this information to generate superior returns."[27]

However, the "evidence" seems to be more manufactured than real. The DJSI analysis includes not only market trends and subjective "environmental performance" – but also reviews of "media, press releases, articles and *stakeholder commentary*" that are often used "as a basis for possible downgrading of a company through the ongoing Media and *Stakeholder* Analysis process" (emphasis added).[28] In other words, even the Dow Jones (!!) Sustainability Index has apparently become yet another activist ally in campaigns against companies that have not gotten onboard the CSR and sustainable development bandwagon.

CERES (the Coalition for Environmentally Responsible Economies) bills itself as "the leading US coalition of environmental, investor and public interest advocacy groups, working together for a sustainable future." It includes some 70 companies that have endorsed the CERES Principles, a ten-point code of environmental conduct, and proudly includes Friends of the Earth, the Rainforest Action Network and Union of Concerned Scientists among its "public interest" members. Its political agenda is plain to see.[29]

Executive director Robert Kinloch Massie's speech on "climate change and fiduciary duty" was displayed prominently on the organization's website throughout 2002, as was the May 2002 Claros report and a similar April 2002 report written for CERES by Innovest Strategic Value Advisors, titled *Value at Risk: Climate Change and the Future of Governance.* All three documents assert that ExxonMobil's stance on climate change could jeopardize long-term shareholder value in the company. They also underscore how closely all these activist groups work together, and in conjunction with other radical organizations like Campaign ExxonMobil. (In fact, CERES was an advisor to the anti-ExxonMobil campaign.) Their common goals are to:

- Pressure company executives to assess "current and probable risk exposure" from climate change policies and link executive compensation to companies' performance on that issue; and
- Compel institutional investors to incorporate climate change considerations into investment strategies, require disclosure of climate change-related information from portfolio companies, increase investments in energy efficiency and renewable energy opportunities, and promote the adoption of government climate change initiatives.

Once again, the documents are laden with glowing recommendations that are long on concepts, unfounded assertions about glittering potential for renewable energy and sustainable development, and horror stories about global warming and "irresponsible" corporations. Frequently written by radical activists, or with their extensive input, the reports are woefully short on facts, figures and solid, independent analysis that meet GAAP standards.

The reports also serve another, equally important role: boosting the value of CERES member companies and investor funds. Boston-based Green Century Funds, for example, invests in companies like AstroPower and Quantum Fuel Systems Technologies, which produce and distribute solar and other renewable energy products. As TechCentralStation.com editor Nick Schulz points out, these firms will profit handsomely if federal and state governments mandate taxpayer subsidies for renewable energy industries, or impose restrictions on greenhouse gas emissions –

thereby generating pressure on utilities and manufacturers to switch to "appropriate" alternative energy systems.

Green Century's Balanced Fund also owns shares in several companies that do not necessarily share its commitment to promote "environmentally sensitive or benign business practices." But by holding 600 shares in BP and 100 in ConocoPhillips (0.02 and 0.003 percent of its portfolio, respectively), the fund qualifies to introduce shareholder resolutions on arctic drilling and other issues at annual meetings.

By investing in Campbell's Soup, Schulz continues, Green Century was able to file a shareholder resolution urging the company to be "socially responsible" by ending its use of genetically modified ingredients. Not mentioned was the fact that two of Green Century's largest holdings are United Natural Foods and Whole Foods Markets, which together enjoyed nearly $4 billion in natural and organic food sales in 2002.[30] Also not mentioned was the adverse impact that this anti-biotechnology pressure continues to have on the poorest people in Africa, Asia and Latin America – or that these same organic food producers and marketers provide millions of dollars a year to the anti-biotech Luddites who conspire to keep the Third World malnourished, susceptible to disease and on the verge of starvation. How socially responsible of them all.

But apparently these broader ethical considerations are beyond the purview and capability of CERES and its members.

The Good Reputation Index evaluates the top 100 companies operating in Australia and New Zealand for supposed socially responsible practices. Gary Johns, coordinator of the Institute of Public Affairs' NGO Project, analyzed its practices. His disturbing findings should serve as a loud alarm for companies, regulators and investors alike – and as a clarion call for financial transparency and accountability for activist NGOs and investor groups.

The Index design was based extensively on input from high-profile NGOs like Greenpeace and Amnesty International, and on the "leading lights of the corporate social responsibility industry."

Objective analyses of financial performance and Index calculations of "social responsibility" are inversely related. Only one of the index's top ten "most socially responsible" corporations is ranked among top 20 companies in terms of financial performance and return on investments. Conversely, only three of the top ten financial performers made the top 20 CSR list. Five of the top ten most socially responsible companies are government-controlled – suggesting that, in the Index's view, government protection is good, and market competition is bad.

Many highly ranked "socially responsible" companies donate heavily to CSR groups, including organizations that act as judges for various CSR indexes. Several of these corporations are also strong promoters of social responsibility and "triple bottom line" dogmas. "One must at least suspect that their high ranking is a reward for their contribution to the cause," notes Johns.[31]

Innovest Strategic Value Advisors is yet another "ethical" investor group. It operates the EcoValue'21 analytical platform and includes among its institutional clients two of the world's largest pension funds, CalPERS in the USA and ABP in the Netherlands.[32]

Innovest recently published "Intangible values linked to sustainability," complementing its *Value at Risk: Climate Change and the Future of Governance* report. Sir Mark Moody-Stuart, former chairman of Royal Dutch/Shell when it initiated WBCSD and other efforts to promote CSR and sustainable development, is now a member of the Innovest board of directors. The group was recently selected to provide company and industry "sustainability" research for BP Investments, the investment arm of the British Petroleum pension fund.[33]

This selection further complicates the spider's web of interrelationships among activist investor advisory groups, liberal foundations and pension funds, radical environmental organizations – and corporations like BP and Shell, which seek to polish their images and profit politically and economically from the sustainability and corporate social responsibility movement that they did so much to inaugurate. It may be part of the reason that BP has managed to retain its preferred status with many "socially responsible" investor groups. (Indeed, in the past, some of these groups also gave high marks to Enron, Global Crossing, WorldCom and other companies that have become virtually synonymous with stock manipulation and investor fraud.)

The United Nations Environmental Programme's Finance Initiatives brings the power of a major government institution into this tangled web. It claims to be a "unique partnership" among the

UNEP and 295 banks, insurance and investment companies, including reinsurance giant Swiss Re – and with a number of radical NGOs like Friends of the Earth and the World Wildlife Fund.

They work hand-in-hand to promote catastrophic global warming theories, arguing that "increasing severe weather events" have resulted in "massive economic losses." The UNEPFI "regards sustainable development as a fundamental aspect of sound business management" and supports the precautionary principle and Kyoto Protocol.

Not surprisingly, these activists hope to mobilize the $26-trillion financial services industry to "wield significant influence over future economic development," and persuade pension funds that they "may see the value of energy or power company holdings decline as investors become more aware of the liabilities linked with carbon-intensive industries."[34] At no time do they acknowledge the paucity of scientific evidence for global warming or the fact that storms are not increasing in number or severity. They also ignore the fact that increasing economic losses from storms and floods are due primarily to expanded construction of expensive homes and buildings in flood plains and along coasts, especially in the United States, over the past several decades.

Fenton Communications, which masterminded the phony 1989 Alar and apples food scare, is viewed by many as a major guiding force behind many of the CSR and SRI campaigns, including clever attacks on genetically improved foods. In 2000 alone, David Fenton and company devised and directed dozens of separate press events, targeting Campbell's Soup, Kellogg's and other companies. Each one promoted junk science, technophobia and, of course, revenue generation for radical attack groups, organic food companies, the mass tort industry and Fenton's other clients.

The accusations are typically groundless, but they resonate with the media, public, politicians – and juries. More importantly for Fenton and his clients, they rake in boatloads of revenue. The Alar scam was a financial bonanza for the Natural Resources Defense Council, a book condemning pesticides brought in nearly $1 million via a 900 number and the "Phil Donohue Show," and the organic food industry has grown by leaps and bounds, thanks in large part to the PR firm's brilliant fear-mongering. In the wake of the Alar campaign alone, claims Fenton, "Lines started forming in health food stores. The sales of organic produce soared. All of which we were very happy about."[35] The NRDC and Fenton's organic food clients were also delighted. The Third World poor, of course, are not nearly so happy.

The startling cooperation and coordination among these groups presents a monumental challenge for the Rule of Law.

• Robert Monks, Institutional Shareholder Services, Claros Consulting, CERES, Innovest, Christian Brothers Investment Services, the DJSI and the UNEP Finance Initiatives provide putative legitimacy and supposedly professional, unbiased analytical and advisory services. They develop computer programs, provide pension fund advisory services, make buy and sell recommendations based on CSR and sustainable development claims, underwrite cursory reviews and questionable analyses, and develop and sell research and advice on proxy voting. All these efforts serve to support a narrow political agenda.
• The activist advisors and a number of major liberal foundations recruit, advise and fund labor unions and liberal church groups like the Interfaith Center on Corporate Responsibility, National Religious Partnership for the Environment and National Council of Churches, often setting agendas and planning strategies.
• They likewise recruit, advise and fund attack groups like Greenpeace and Campaign ExxonMobil, bringing their motley assortment of radicals and anarchists into play.
• Government agencies, especially at the federal level, provide further research in support of activist causes and millions of dollars in direct financial assistance to activist groups, as well as regulatory pressure in support of their agendas.[36]
• All work in consort to develop radical new principles of corporate ethics and government control, while pressuring corporations, legislators and regulators to adopt their vision and agenda – based on false, misleading, make-believe notions about resource depletion, planetary destruction, renewable energy, sustainable development, precaution, food safety, global warming and social responsibility.

• All support activities that seek to promote the reputation and value of favored companies and politicians, while damaging the good name and bottom line of those that have not yet "seen the light" on CSR, sustainable development, the precautionary principle and global warming.
• Beneficiary corporations – like members of CERES, the WBCSD and the UNEPFI – hope to profit from being associated with the "green hats." They may seek competitive advantages, or hope to reduce public censure for their roles in "resource depletion and environmental degradation." Often, they are persuaded to embark on product development programs (such as electric cars) that may be politically attractive in the near term, but are fraught with serious technological and economic questions, and thus raise serious questions regarding the companies' fiduciary duties to investors and creditors.

As the Enron stain continues to spread, questions have arisen regarding additional examples of *corporate* abuses – such as potential conflicts of interest, lack of arms-length relationships and misleading statements that have led consumers to believe they were dealing with independent associations offering advice about insurance or other products. In one case involving an insurance company, complainants charged that, "far from being independent, many of these associations serve primarily as a marketing arm" for particular insurers or agencies, endorsing their products to the exclusion of others.[37]

The 2002 Sarbanes-Oxley Act demands that a massive wall be erected to separate analysts from investor bankers. It also forces Wall Street firms (and thus investors) to spend millions on "independent" research, and imposes civil and criminal sanctions for a wide range of misdeeds and mistakes. However, it does absolutely nothing to address the collusion, misrepresentations, conflicts of interest and secretive, convoluted relationships involving nonprofit activist groups.

In fact, in this post-Enron era, nearly every conceivable buyer-seller, consumer-merchant, public-corporate relationship is being scrutinized infinitely more closely than ever before. But the equally troubling and far-reaching relationships detailed here are still exempt from review and from legislative, regulatory or judicial action.

No one is suggesting that environmental activist organizations should not have a right to organize, speak out and promote their cause. However, they should do so in accord with the laws, regulations and ethical guidelines that govern for-profit businesses and trade associations. The potential for this cartel of special interest organizations to manipulate markets and prices, pressure companies and consumers, mislead investors and violate numerous codes of ethics is enormous. Their conflict of interest is real and obvious. Their integrity is on the line.

It is time for Robert Monks, Claros Consulting, Campaign ExxonMobil and all their allied groups to come clean. To do what they demand of for-profit corporations. To open their books and provide full disclosure of their meetings, contacts, monetary and other relationships, direct and indirect. To act in accord with false advertising laws, and abide by accepted standards of honesty, integrity and accountability.

If they have nothing to hide, they should be happy to disclose and broadcast these facts and relationships for all to see. Their reluctance to open their books and come clean about their activities and relationships strongly suggests that they have much to hide.

It is also time for Congress, state legislatures, regulators, journalists and watchdog groups to hold hearings, investigate these organizations and their operations, and ensure that all operate in accord with the same rules and principles that now govern for-profit corporations and the rest of our civilized society. These true watchdogs need to exercise their jurisdiction and meet their obligations to the taxpaying and investing public – to ensure full scrutiny, full transparency, full public disclosure and full accountability, under the principles articulated by *Fortune*, *Business Week* and other observers.

How can responsible citizens help to stop the charade? For starters, demand that corporate social responsibility puts people first, puts development back into sustainable development, and ensures that precautionary guidelines safeguard people and communities from the havoc wreaked by radical green policies.

Insist that all decisions be based on sound, peer-reviewed science and solid evidence – not on hysterical claims and shrill rhetoric by activists, regulators and journalists, who reward pseudoscientific soul-mates and pillory any scientists, economists or financial analysts who dare to disagree with them.

Urge principled regulators and journalists to investigate these companies and investor firms for self-serving arrangements and breech of fiduciary duty. Demand that the companies, firms and activist groups open their books and provide full disclosure of their meetings, contacts, and monetary, political and other relationships.

Last, in this era of high-minded reform, prevail upon legislators to change the law, to make these groups subject to the same false advertising laws, and the same standards of transparency and accountability, that activists and politicians insist should govern for-profit corporations.

The world will be a better, safer, more ethical place – especially for energy and resource consumers, taxpayers, voters, retirees, and the world's poor.

Chapter Ten Footnotes

1. See Paul Craig Roberts, "Criminalizing business" [with the Sarbanes-Oxley corporate reform law], *Washington Times*, October 23, 2002; Jack Kemp, "Criminalizing corporate behavior," *Washington Times*, October 30, 2002; Neil Weinberg, "Criminalizing Capitalism: Politicians are punishing Wall Street to avenge a stock market gone sour. Main Street and small investors will be among the unintended victims," *Forbes*, May 12, 2003.
2. Joseph Nocera, "System Failure: Corporate America has lost its way. Here's a road map for restoring confidence," *Fortune*, June 24, 2002. These suggestions originated with a June 6, 2002 report by the NY Stock Exchange.
3. John A. Byrne, *et al.*, "Restoring trust in corporate America: Business must lead the way to real reform," *Business Week*, June 24, 2002.
4. *Ibid.*
5. Rich Long, "Countering Corporate Arrogance," *The Public Relations Strategist*, Spring 2002 – quoting Carole Gorney, director of Lehigh University's Center for Crisis Public Relations and Litigation Studies.
6. Joseph Nocera, "System Failure."
7. *Ibid.* See also Mark Gunther, "Investors of the world, unite! It's up to institutional investors to fix corporate America, says the dean of shareholder activists," *Fortune*, June 24, 2002.
8. John A. Byrne, "Restoring trust in corporate America."
9. Joseph Nocera, "System Failure"; "How to fix Wall Street," *Washington Post* editorial, November 11, 2002; John A. Byrne, "Restoring trust in corporate America;" John C. Bogle, "Reality Bites," *Wall Street Journal*, November 21, 2002. Otherwise, they say, especially in the case of IPOs, analysts too easily serve as a marketing tool, implicitly (and sometimes explicitly) promising favorable coverage if their firm is allowed to underwrite the deal.
10. Mark Gunther, "Investors of the world, unite!" – citing shareholder activist Robert A.G. Monks. See also John A. Byrne, *et al.*, "How to fix corporate governance," *Business Week*, May 6, 2002
11. See Charles R. Schwab, "My investors, my responsibility," *Wall Street Journal,* November 5, 2002. See also Gary Johns, "Protocols with NGOs: The need to know," *IPA Backgrounder*, Institute of Public Affairs (Melbourne, Australia), October 2001. This report and other work by Johns examine how the increased standing and power granted to non-governmental organization "stakeholders" in recent years has resulted in other citizens having reduced standing and muted voices – particularly when the NGOs enjoy both tax exempt status and government subsidies. The report recommends several "protocols" to restore transparency and accountability to the system.

12. Joseph Nocera, "System Failure"; John A. Byrne, "How to fix corporate governance." See also Jarol Manheim, "Biz-War: Origins, structure and strategy of foundation-NGO network warfare on corporations in the United States," paper presented at June 11, 2003 conference on NGOs, American Enterprise Institute, Washington, DC (www.aei.org).
13. Mark Gunther, "Investors of the world, unite!"
14. Personal communication from Ray Bohlin to Paul Driessen, June 4, 2002. Father Crosby had similarly harsh words for this author, accusing him of "ad hominem attacks" for challenging statements and resolutions presented by him, Sister Pat Daly, Robert Monks, CERES and other shareholder activists at the 2004 ExxonMobil annual meeting. He was particularly incensed that anyone would question the activists scientific claims or suggest that their political agenda violates the human rights of poor people in developing countries. The fact that Harry Alford, president of the National Black Chamber of Commerce, Reverend John Nunes and Reverend Jerry Zandstra also criticized the activists only increased Father Crosby's ire.
15. Capital Research Center, *Foundation Watch* newsletter, "Explorations in Nonprofits: Part II: Environmentalists Gain Ground" (2002).
16. Mark Gunther, "Investors of the world, unite!"
17. Mark Mansley, *Risking Shareholder Value? ExxonMobil and Climate Change: An Investigation of Unnecessary Risks and Missed Opportunities,* Claros Consulting, May 2002. Available on the Claros, CERES and Campaign ExxonMobil websites.
18. Mark Gunther, "Investors of the world, unite!"
19. Jeffrey Ball, "Global warming threatens health of corporations," *Wall Street Journal,* April 16, 2003.
20. Wall Street Journal editorial, "Where the Money Is," February 24, 2003; Gary Johns, "Corporate Social Responsibility or Civil Society Regulation?" page 7.
21. See http://www.claros.pwp.blueyonder.co.uk
22. Transcript of May 2, 2002, teleconference featuring Peter Altman, National Coordinator of Campaign Exxon Mobil; Mark Mansley of Claros Consulting of London, England; Arianne Buren, Senior Project Manager of the Sustainable Governance Project at CERES; and shareholder activist, Robert A.G. Monks. Transcript is available at www.hastingsgroup.com/shareholderstudy.html.
23. "The Best Big Companies in America: The Forbes Platinum 400 have the best balance of long- and short-term financial performance," *Forbes,* January 6, 2003.
24. Ironically, another paragon of sustainability and corporate social responsibility, Royal Dutch/Shell, was caught misstating its oil and gas reserves in 2004. From the company's report on how this

happened, "the most amazing lapse leaps out. Get this: The world's No. 2 energy producer [had] relied on a lone former employee to audit its annual estimate of reserves – and he worked part-time." The auditor noted that he had stopped questioning suspicious numbers some years before, because operating unit executives would object any time he raised a red flag. Robert Barker, "Keeping hot air out of energy reserves," *Business Week*, May 10, 2004.

25. See Marc Morano, "Oil giant 'guilty of crimes against humanity,' protesters say," Media Research Center, www.green-watch.com, May 29, 2002.

26. Activist watchdog Ron Arnold, commenting on www.undue-influence.com/exxon_mobil_attacks.htm. The UndueInfluence website is a useful resource for "tracking the environmental movement's money, power and harm," as it uses "capitalist invest-ments to destroy capitalist society." The site includes a "master page" on the ExxonMobil attack campaigns and extensive information about numerous activist foundations and radical groups.

27. See www.sustainability-indexes.com and the February 2002 *DJSI Newsletter,* page 2.

28. See *Dow Jones STOXX Sustainability Indexes Guide,* version 2.0, September 2002, page 13, available on the DJSI website. See also Steven Hayward, "The new corporate balance sheet: Black, red – and green," American Enterprise Institute, *Environmental Policy Outlook*, October 2002, http://www.aei.org/epo/epo14483.htm

29. See www.ceres.org and Nick Schulz, "Gaia and Greenbacks," TechCentralStation.com, May 28, 2003.

30. Nick Schulz, "Gaia and Greenbacks." See also Jon Entine, "Capitalism's Trojan Horse: How the 'social investment' movement undermines stakeholder relations and emboldens the anti-free market activities of NGOs," paper presented at June 11, 2003 conference on NGOs, American Enterprise Institute, Washington, DC (www.aei.org).

31. Gary Johns, "Corporate Social Responsibility or Civil Society Regulation?" page 6.

32. ABP is the pension fund for the Netherlands' government and educational employees.

33. See www.innovest.com

34. UNEP Finance Initiatives press release, "Financial sector, governments and business must act on climate change or face the consequences," October 8, 2002; "UNEP Statement by Financial Institutions on the Environment and Sustainable Development," A s Revised, May 1997, http://unepfi.net/fii/english.htm

35. See Bonner Cohen, John Carlisle, *et al., The Fear Profiteers: Do "socially responsible" businesses sow health scares to reap*

monetary rewards? Arlington, VA: Lexington Institute (2000); "Who's Running the Anti-Biotech Public Relations Machine?" Center for Consumer Freedom, October 1, 2000; Jay Byrne, "Money, Marketing and the Internet: Unanticipated and Unacknowledged Factors Influencing Agricultural Biotechnology Public Acceptance," American Enterprise Institute, June 2003 (from conference on "Biotechnology, the Media and Public Policy").

36. See Henry Lamb, "How the feds hand out your dollars," WorldNetDaily, December 7, 2002. Lamb calculates that just six environmental organizations (including the World Resources Institute, National Audubon Society, World Wildlife Fund and NRDC) received $129.1 million in taxpayer dollars between 1997 and 2001. The Nature Conservancy alone received $146.7 million in addition to what these six got. An additional $25 million went to several government organizations and labor unions, including $4.4 million to the American Federation of State, County and Municipal Employees, which in turn contributed $19.5 million to political candidates – 98 percent of it to Democrats. (Under current law, unions are not required to conduct independent audits of their accounting books and financial records. However, proposed Department of Labor rules would mandate that unions keep records of money spent each year on political and lobbying activities, as well as on organizing and strike benefits.) See also Marc Morano, "EPA seeks faith-based grants for green causes," CNSNews.com, December 20, 2002; Hugo Gurdon, "The Grim Green Giant: The environmentalist establishment's lobbying behemoth," *CEI's Monthly Planet*, January 2003; Ivan Osorio, "The Greens' Federal Cash Grab," *CEI's Monthly Planet*, March 2003, available online at www.CEI.org; Max Primorac, "Funding anti-US Demonstrators: State Department grants are questionable," *Washington Times*, May 2, 2003.

37. Chad Terhune, "Nonprofit groups that tout insurance have hidden links: Associations that offer deals are often set up by insurers; rate boosts come later," *Wall Street Journal*, November 21, 2001.

11

End of Eco-Imperialism?

Some 60,000 activists, bureaucrats and politicians flew gas-guzzling, greenhouse-gas-spewing jets into Johannesburg, South Africa, in August 2002 for a $50-million Earth Summit. Many settled into comfy five-star hotels, intending to make the summit a high water mark for sustainable development, global warming and the precautionary principle.

Over the next two weeks, many of them denounced everything from electricity and flush toilets, to fossil fuels, biotechnology, capitalism and, of course, the United States. The World Wildlife Fund issued a jeremiad, wailing that mankind will need at least 1.2 more Planet Earths by 2050 to maintain our present standard of living, if people don't change their evil ways.

However, despite their titanic efforts, the summit didn't turn out quite the way they expected.

The United States, Australia and Canada refused to go along with the orchestrated agenda and, instead, promoted free markets, free trade and economic development as the solution to global poverty and environmental degradation. Secretary of State Collin Powell spoke eloquently in support of these themes and the three nations' increasing alliance with the developing countries against the forces of pessimism and alarmism. USAID Director Andrew Natsios spoke out against NGO and EU demands that starving people be denied genetically modified corn.

Writing in London's *Telegraph*, Leon Louw, director of South Africa's Free Market Foundation, accused the NGOs and EU of "insidious eco-imperialism." These "neo-Luddites," he argued, "place elitist environmental whims and nebulous conceptions about 'resource depletion' above the needs of the world's destitute billions. They seek to impose first-world concepts of environmentalism and human development ... on developing countries. They do not want poor countries to follow the path that made the prosperity of their own countries possible."[1]

"Anti-development and anti-trade" policies, said Louw, at their core are "anti-human."

The charges resonated. Developing nations openly rebelled against the "sustainable development" agenda. Hundreds of poor African protesters marched in Johannesburg against what they called the politics and policies of "Sustained Poverty." Their growing anger and resentment toward "green despotism" was obvious.

Barun Mitra of India presented a special "BS Award" to the international NGOs for "sustaining poverty." It was a plaque heaped high with two piles of animal excrement – symbolizing both the quality of the environmental radicals' arguments and the "biomass" fuel that many NGOs seem to want poverty-stricken Third World families to use for generations to come.[2]

Free Africa Foundation president George Ayittey condemned the corruption endemic in many of the governments attending the Johannesburg summit. "What exists in many African countries," he says, "is a 'vampire' or 'pirate' state – a government hijacked by a phalanx of gangsters, thugs and crooks who use the instruments of the state to enrich themselves, their cronies," their tribesmen, and various bureaucrats and educated elites. The poor get almost nothing – and little of the aid promised at the first sustainability conference in Rio de Janeiro has ever materialized. No wonder Africa's villagers and honest politicians have become so disenchanted with attempts to impose First World treaties and policies on the Third World, he suggested.[3]

In the end, many of the greens' key agenda items were tabled, voted down or relegated to indeterminate timetables, and they were left to cry in their white wine. The Energy and Climate Caucus coalition denounced the Earth summit as a "total failure," Friends of the Earth called it "notably feeble," and Oxfam International summed it up as "nine days of bluster."[4]

It is certainly dangerous to make any kind of prediction about the demise of an $8-billion-a-year global environmental gorilla. However, it is possible that Johannesburg will turn out to have been a watershed event in the history of eco extremism.

At previous summits dating back to 1992 in Rio de Janeiro, discussions had focused on Malthusian limits to growth, planetary apocalypse and global governance. In Johannesburg, the focus was on poverty – and on how poverty can be eliminated, and people's health and environmental quality improved, through private property rights, market economies, global trade, technology, innovation, democratic processes, sustained economic growth, and the right of individuals, communities and nations to make their own decisions and chart their own destinies.

At previous summits, the dominant theme was the struggle between rich and poor ... between haves and have-nots ... between a "greedy" United States and an impoverished Third World. In Johannesburg, the struggle was largely between those whose vision is one of hope, progress and faith in mankind's amazing intellectual capacity – against those whose vision is one of fear, worsening environmental degradation and man as the supreme danger to all he surveys.

Whether this change in priorities and agendas becomes permanent is largely up to those who support Third World rights of self-determination. The task will not be easy, but it can be done. To maintain the momentum, they must:

• Challenge BP, Shell and other companies, politicians, bureaucrats, journalists and investor groups to rediscover their moral compass and do the right thing – on energy and economic development, corporate social responsibility, sustainable economic development and reasonable precaution. Third World advocates can do so not only by appealing to the more moderate organizations' better instincts, but also by publicly embarrassing the more radical elements for their human rights abuses.

• Insist that the same laws and ethical principles apply to all corporations – for-profit and not-for-profit alike. Demand that NGOs, and the foundations and government agencies that fund them, be required to abide by the same principles of honesty, integrity, transparency, disclosure and accountability that they have long demanded for the corporate world.
• Confront the persistent socialist ideologies and government infrastructures that still dominate much of Europe, Africa, Asia and the United Nations.
• Find new ways to broaden the public discourse in these arenas, where free speech, true press diversity, talk radio, think tanks, internet access and other independent sources of thought are far less prevalent than in the United States and Australia.
• Provide greater financial and other support to think tanks, journalists, politicians, companies and other advocates of private property, free markets, trade, technology, innovation, democracy and economic growth.
• Recruit and support more people in developing countries who want an opportunity to be heard. Give them forums to confront the radical NGOs and urge market reforms that offer the greatest hope for better futures for families and communities in developing countries.
• Concentrate on providing energy, jobs, economic opportunities, and better health and environmental quality for people in developing countries. Reduce the focus on government aid programs and give less credence to the claims and agendas of high-pressure activist groups.

Do these things, and Johannesburg could mark, not just a pothole, but the end of the road for eco-imperialism – and new hope for millions of the world's poor.

Chapter Eleven Footnotes

1. Leon Louw, "Poverty today is truly miraculous," *London Telegraph*, January 9, 2002.
3. During the 2003 World Trade Organization Ministerial Summit in Cancun, Mexico, the Congress of Racial Equality used an Academy Awards format to present "Green Power-Black Death" awards to organizations that it determined were most responsible for bringing misery and death to developing countries. Greenpeace, the European Union and Malaysia-based Pesticide Action Network took top "dis-honors" in their respective categories. See Paul Driessen, "CORE mocks environmentalists in Cancun," *Environment & Climate News*, January 2004, page 9 (www.heartland.org).
3. George B. Ayittey, "Why Africa is poor," in *Sustainable Development: Promoting progress or perpetuating poverty?* Julian Morris (editor), London: Profile Books (2002). See also Thompson Ayodele, "Malaria: Saving lives and protecting the environment," www.IPPANigeria.org, June 10, 2003. Ayodele, director of Nigeria's Institute of Public Policy Analysis, summarizes the ways this disease keeps Nigeria and other African countries impoverished.
3. Marc Morano, "Earth Summit's Failure Called 'Good Thing' For Poor Nations," CNSNews.com, September 5, 2002.

Eco-Imperialism

12

Corporate Social Responsibility Reborn

Ideas and ideologies have consequences. Horrid ideas and ideologies have lethal consequences.

From their very beginnings, activist doctrines of corporate social responsibility have too narrowly defined what is moral, ethical, sustainable, ecologically beneficial, compassionate or in the public interest. Since the doctrines first emerged, companies, journalists and politicians have treated the views and demands of CSR activists and other hostile critics of business as more rationally based, more representative of "society's expectations," more morally sound, than they really are.

Under what standards – by whose definition – is it moral, ethical or socially responsible to deny the world's most destitute people the benefits that people in the developing world have long enjoyed from energy development, malaria prevention, biotech foods and freedom to trade? How can people of good conscience allow assertions, accusations and agendas of ideological extremists to become the arbiter of corporate and societal responsibility?

161

Free markets and free people generate optimism, opportunity, innovation, prosperity, health and environmental quality. But eco-centric CSR activists demand one vision, one mode of thought, one doctrine of ethical, economic and environmental policy – all in the service of an ideology of pessimism, scarcity and indifference to the plight of billions. They permit no marketplace of ideas, no deviation from their mode of thinking, no right of people in different companies, communities, cultures and countries to think for themselves, make their own decisions, set their own priorities, address their own pressing problems, decide their own destinies.

At best, their blind adherence to current CSR doctrine puts the European Union, United Nations, many journalists and World Business Council for Sustainable Development members like BP and Shell in league with some of the most radical elements of Western society. At worst, it makes them guilty of silent complicity (or even active collaboration) in the misery and death of millions.

The need for reform is clear. Responsible companies and politicians must demonstrate real leadership, reexamine the tenets of corporate social responsibility, and alter their stance on this radical doctrine. They must show that they truly care about people – and not just about profiting from policies sanctioned by CSR doctrines, or burnishing their reputations among Euro, green, Hollywood and media elites.

They need to lead the way in making the world a better place for its poorest inhabitants, by challenging radical ideologues on their anti-poor policies. They need to insist that doctrines of corporate social responsibility, sustainable economic development, caution and ethical investing reflect the needs of people, especially the poorest citizens of our planet.

As C.S. Lewis observed:

> "Of all tyrannies, a tyranny exercised for the good of its victims may be the most oppressive. It may be better to live under robber barons than under omnipotent moral busybodies. The robber baron's cruelty may sometimes sleep, his cupidity may at some point be satiated; but those who torment us for our own good will torment us without end, for they do so with the approval of their own conscience."[1]

Chapter Twelve Footnotes

1. C.S. Lewis, "The Humanitarian Theory of Punishment," in *God in the Dock: Essays on Theology and Ethics,* by C. S. Lewis, edited by Walter Hooper, William B. Eerdmans Publishing Company, Grand Rapids, Michigan, 1970, p. 292. "The Humanitarian Theory of Punishment" first appeared in *20th Century: An Australian Quarterly Review,* vol. III, No. 3 (1949), pp. 5-12. Philosopher, physicist and author C. P. Snow offered his own succinct commentary on moral and environmental imperialism. "Industrialization is the only hope of the poor," he wrote. "It is all very well for us, sitting pretty, to think that material standards of living don't matter all that much. It is all very well for one, as a personal choice, to reject industrialization – do a moden Walden, if you like; and if you go without much food, see most of your children die in infancy, accept twenty years off your own life, then I respect you for the strength of your aesthetic revulsion. But I don't respect you in the slightest if, even passively, you try to impose the same choice on others who are not free to choose. In fact, we know what their choice would be. For, with singular unanimity, in any country where they have had the chance, the poor have walked off the land into factories as fast as the factories could take them." *The Two Cultures: And a Second Look,* New York: New American Library (1963), page 30.

Eco-Imperialism

Bibliography

Adler, Jonathan H., editor; *The Costs of Kyoto: Climate change policy and its implications*; Washington, DC: Competitive Enterprise Institute (1997).

Arnold, Ron; *Ecology Wars: Environmentalism As If People Mattered*; Bellevue, WA: Free Enterprise Press (1987).

Arnold, Ron; *Undue Influence: Wealthy foundations, grant-driven environmental groups, and zealous bureaucrats that control your future*; Bellevue, WA: Free Enterprise Press (1999).

Avery, Dennis; *Saving the Planet with Pesticides and Plastic*; Indianapolis, IN: Hudson Institute (2000).

Bailey, Ronald; *Global Warming and Other Eco-Myths: How the environmental movement uses false science to scare us to death*; Washington, DC: Competitive Enterprise Institute (2002), Bailey, Ronald, editor; *Earth Report 2000: Revisiting the True State of the Planet*; New York: McGraw Hill (2000).

Bast, Joseph L., Peter J. Hill and Richard C. Rue; *Eco-Sanity: A commonsense guide to environmentalism*; Lanham, MD: Madison Books (1994; second edition 1996).

Bastiat, Frederic; *The Law*; Irvington-on-Hudson, NY: Foundation for Economic Freedom (1950).

Beckerman, Wilfred; *A Poverty of Reason: Sustainable development and economic growth"*; Oakland, CA: The Independent Institute (2002).

Bradley, Robert L. Jr.; *Julian Simon and the Triumph of Energy Sustainability*; Washington, DC: American Legislative Exchange Council (2000).

Bradley, Robert L. Jr.; *Climate Alarmism Reconsidered*; London: Institute of Economic Affairs (2003). Bradley is president of the Institute for Energy Research, Houston, Texas.

DeGregori, Thomas; *Bountiful Harvest: Technology, food safety and the environment*; Washington, DC: Cato Institute (2002).

DeSoto, Hernando; *The Mystery of Capital: Why capitalism triumphs in the West and fails everywhere else*; New York: Basic Books (2000).

Desowitz, Robert S., *The Malaria Capers: Tales of parasites and people*; New York: W. W. Norton & Company (1991).

Easterbrook, Gregg; *A Moment on the Earth: The coming age of environmental optimism*; New York: Viking Books (1995).

Fagan, Brian; *The Little Ice Age: How climate made history, 1300-1850;* New York: Basic Books (2000).

Friedmann, John and Haripriya Rangan; editors; *In Defense of Livelihood: Comparative Studies on Environmental Action;* West Hartford, CT.: Kumarian Press (1993).

Fumento, Michael; *Science Under Siege: Balancing Technology and the Environment*; New York: William Morrow and Company, Inc. (1993).

Goklany, Indur M.; *Economic Growth and the State of Humanity*; Bozeman, MT: Political Economy Research Center (2001).

Hagen, Eric W. and James J. Worman; *An Endless Series of Hobgoblins: The Science and Politics of Environmental Health Scares*; Irvington-on-Hudson: Foundation for Economic Education (1995).

Henderson, David; *Misguided Virtue: False notions of corporate responsibility,* London: Institute of Economic Affairs (2001).

Huber, Peter; *Galileo's Revenge: Junk Science in the Courtroom*; New York: Basic Books (1991).

Johns, Gary; "Corporate Social Responsibility or Civil Society Regulation?" Melbourne, Australia: Institute of Public Affairs, Hal Clough Lecture (2002).

Johns, Gary; "Protocols with NGOs: The Need to Know"; Melbourne, Australia: Institute of Public Affairs, IPA Backgrounder, Vol. 13/1 (2001).

Juberg, Daland; *Are Children More Vulnerable to Environmental Chemicals? Scientific and Regulatory Issues in Perspective;* New York: American Council on Science and Health (2003).

Lomborg, Bjorn; *The Skeptical Environmentalist: Measuring the real state of the world;* Cambridge: Cambridge University Press (2001).

Michaels, Patrick J. and Robert C. Balling, Jr.; *The Satanic Gases: Clearing the air about global warming;* Washington, DC: Cato Institute (2000).

Milloy, Steven and Michael Gough; *Silencing Science;* Washington, DC: Cato Institute (1999).

Mitra, Barun and Richard Tren; *The Burden of Malaria;* Delhi, India: Liberty Institute, Occasional Paper 12 (2002).

Moore, Stephen, Julian Simon and Rita Simon; *It's Getting Better All the Time: 100 greatest trends of the last 100 years;* Washington, DC: Cato Institute (2000).

Morris, Julian; *Sustainable Development: Promoting progress or perpetuating poverty?* London: Profile Books (2002).

Narayan, Deepa; *Voices of the Poor: Can Anyone Hear Us?* Oxford: Oxford University Press (2000).

Neal, Mark and Christie Davies; *The Corporation under Siege: Exposing the devices used by activists and regulators in the non-risk society;* London: Social Affairs Unit (1998).

Nichols, Nick; *Rules for Corporate Warriors: How to fight and survive attack group shakedowns;* Bellevue, WA: Merril Press (2001).

Norberg, Johann; *In Defence of Global Capitalism;* Stockholm, Sweden: Timbro (2001).

Paarlberg, Robert; *The Politics of Precaution: Genetically modified crops in developing countries;* Baltimore, MD: Johns Hopkins University Press (2001).

Pomerantz, Kenneth and Steven Topik; *The World that Trade Created: Society, culture and the world economy: 1400 to the present;* Armonk, NY: M. E. Sharpe (1999).

Prasad, Rayasam; *Collapse of a Dream: Social effects of economics in India and the world;* Pittsburgh, PA: CeShore Publishing Company (2001).

Rangan, Haripriya; *Of Myths and Movements: Rewriting Chipko into Himalayan History;* New York: Verso (2000).

Rosenberg, Nathan and L.E. Birdzell; *How the West Grew Rich: The economic transformation of the industrial world*; New York: Basic Books (1986).

Schall, James Vincent; *Religion, Wealth and Poverty*; Vancouver, BC: Fraser Institute (1990).

Sheehan, James; *Global Greens: Inside the International Environmental Establishment*; Washington, DC: Capital Research Center (1998). Includes appendix of environmental advocacy organizations and major foundation grants to them.

Simon, Julian; *The Ultimate Resource 2: Natural resources, pollution, world's food supply, pressures of population growth. Every trend in material human welfare has been improving and promises to continue to do so, indefinitely*; Princeton, NJ: Princeton University Press (1998).

Sternberg, Elaine; *Corporate Governance: Accountability in the marketplace*; London: Institute of Economic Affairs (1998).

Tren, Richard and Roger Bate; *When Politics Kills: Malaria and the DDT story*; Sandton, South Africa: Africa Fighting Malaria (2000).

Walberg, Herbert J. and Joseph L. Bast; *Education and Capitalism: How overcoming our fear of markets and economics can improve America's schools*; Stanford, CA: Hoover Institution Press (2003).

Williams, Walter E.; *More Liberty Means Less Government: Our founders knew this well*; Stanford, CA: Hoover Institution Press, No. 453 (1999).

Videotapes and DVDs

Against Nature; Martin Durkin producer, London: Channel 4 Television Corporation (1997).

Harvest of Fear; Jon Palfreman producer; Boston: WGBH Educational Foundation, NOVA and Frontline (2001).

Penn & Teller: Bullshit! New York: Viacom Company and Showtime Entertainment (2004). DVD collection includes "Eat This!" and "Environmental Hysteria" episodes.

Index

A

accountability of companies and nonprofit groups, 8, 11-14, *17n*, 78, 124, 131-134, 136, 144, 149, 150, *151n*, 158.
Adam Smith, 5, 82.
Agenda 21, 7, 83.
Alar chemical scare, 146.
Alaska Wilderness League, 11.
American Medical Association, 53.
American Wind Energy Association, 89.
Amnesty International, 12, 25, 74, 144.
Annan, Kofi, 7.
Arctic National Wildlife Refuge (ANWR), 95, 117-119.
Argentina, 48, 81, 120, 137.
Arnold, Ron, *x*, *114n*,142, *152n.*
Arntzen, Dr. Charles, 58.
Asian brown cloud, 39.
Audubon Society, 41, 89, *153n.*
Avery, Dennis, *ix*, 58, *64n.*
Ayittey, George, 156.

B

BP *(see British Petroleum).*
bananas, 47, 48, *62n.*
Bangladesh, 67, 78.
Basel Convention on Hazardous Wastes, 80, 108.
Bate, Roger, *ix*, 25, *33n*, *75n*, *76n.*
Beckerman, Wilfred, *16n*, 27, *33n.*
bed nets, 68, 71, 69.
Begley, Ed, 35, *41n*, 70.
Beyond Petroleum ad campaign, 3-5, *16n*, 88, *96n*, *112n*, 116, 117, *126n.*
Bichel Committee on organic farming, *64n.*
biosafety protocol, 48, 49.
biotechnology, *vii*, 22, 24, 28, *32n*, 47-49, 51, 53-56, 58-61, *62n-64n*, 108, 123, 124, 135, 144, *153n*, 155.
benefits of, 51, 53, 55, 56, 58-61, 124.
Bt corn, 50, 57.

Eco-Imperialism

Washington Post, 11, *17n*, *62n*,
129, *151n*.
Washington Times, *43n*, *62n*, *75n*,
76n, *97n*, *113n*, *114n*, 116,
126n, *127n*, *151n*, *154n*.
waste-to-energy plants, 92.
West Nile virus, 73
Whole Foods Markets, 144.
wind power, 3, 4, 35, 37-42, *44n*,
87-91, 94, 95, *96n*, 104, 116,
117, 122, *127n*.
World Bank, 69, 83, 84.
World Business Council for Sustainable Development, 8, *18n*,
22, *32n*, 74, 100, 117, 162.
World Health Organization, 38,
56, 66, 67, 69, 70, *75n*, *76n*,
83, 86.

Z
Zambia, 45, 46, 48, 67, *75n*.
Zhou, Kate, 80, *85n*.
Zimbabwe, 47, 48, 71.
Zoellick, Robert, 45, 55, *62n*,
63n.

Eco-Imperialism

Accolades for *Eco-Imperialism* and Paul Driessen

"If you want to listen to the voice of the poor on environmental issues, read *Eco-Imperialism*. The poor of the world are tired of being led and dictated to by do-gooders who seem determined to keep them mired in poverty for their own selfish ideological and fundraising reasons. This book offers a platform for the voiceless and kicks off a debate that will help facilitate homegrown solutions to Third World problems."

James Shikwati, Inter-Region Economic Network Kenya

"My hope is that the Driessen book, along with work being done at a number of think tanks and by some other groups, will help wake more people up to how the good intentions of some extreme environmentalists have been paving the way to something hellish for many in the Third World."

Jay Ambrose chief editorial writer,
Scripps Howard News Service.

"Telling destitute people in my country, and in countries with even greater destitution, that they must never aspire to living standards much better than they have now - because it wouldn't be 'sustainable' - is just one example of the hypocrisy we have had thrust in our faces, in an era when we can and should grow fast enough to become fully developed in a single generation. We're fed up with it, and gladdened that Driessen and others are taking up our cause. This book could mark a watershed event in environmental politics, and should be read (and absorbed) by all decent people who truly want to be 'socially responsible.'"

Leon Louw, Free Market Foundation of South Africa

"*Eco-Imperialism* is a shocking, profound and desperately needed account of what happens when the privileged Western world decides the fate of millions of people whom they never have to see or hear. Driessen sees and hears, and shares it all."

Sterling Rome, United States

"If you are a modern day environmentalist, you will hate this book. But if you are on the side of humanity and the world's destitute masses, this book will shock, anger and enlighten you, as it disputes the current accepted wisdom about environmental ethics."

Rolf Penner, Canada (South-East Agripost)

"The DDT story is one example of environmental activism taken to an extreme and horrific outcome. The model of environmental activism consisted of fabrications, selective use or outright misuse of science, legal actions, intimidation of scientists and corporations, civil disobedience, and an absolute conviction that all political, covert and unethical methods were justified in order to achieve a greater good. The same model is used today, even as the horrible consequences of environmental actions become increasingly apparent. Driessen is correct. It is high time that environmental organizations be held to standards already demanded of for-profit-corporations: namely, ethical conduct, respect for scientific accuracy, accountability and transparency."

Donald R. Roberts, PhD,
professor of tropical public health, USA

"Paul Driessen's challenging new book recalls the final words of Anna Bramwell's little 1994 masterpiece, *The Fading of the Greens*: the environment is the 'Northern White Empire's last burden, and may be its last crusade.'"

Philip Stott, emeritus professor of biogeography,
University of London

"Paul Driessen forcefully makes the case that the environmental movement has been needlessly anti-human. The real moral and technical challenge is to save both planet and people, and we've been given the intelligence and societal skills to do it."

Dennis Avery,
Center for Global Food Issues, USA

"I am watching your University of Wisconsin presentation on C-SPAN 2 'Book TV.' I am a Liberian and a graduate of UMASS Boston with a degree in Management Information Systems. I will buy your book. Your position on how to help poorer countries of the world develop is just what we need!!!! As you know, we are just recovering from 14 years of civil wars, but some of the material you just talked about on TV could go a long way of helping my people, especially with our great need for electricity, modern farming and education about these issues. I will also recommend your book to other Liberians, so that we can work together using some of your ideas. Maybe someday when Liberia is stabilized, we will invite you to speak at the University of Liberia."

Wilmot Bright, Liberia

"There is a shrill claim today by those who fill the streets to protest globalization, and by the organizations that put them there, that these white, relatively affluent groups are speaking on behalf of the world's poor and powerless. This unfortunately, is a message that the Western media have bought uncritically - but not Paul Driessen. He cogently shows how the new Green Eco-Imperialists are seeking to impose their will on developing countries, interfering with their efforts to build dams or grow crops or do any of the things which can lift them out of poverty. These are life-and-death matters for the world's poor, and Driessen is bold and honest enough to challenge the eco-interference in people's lives as immoral and the cause of death and devastation in countries that are trying to develop and transform their lives. Both those who have bought the Green propaganda line and those who have not would benefit from reading Driessen's *Eco-Imperialism* book."

Thomas R. DeGregori, PhD, Professor of Economics, University of Houston

"A developing country does not need First World ideological oppression. It needs to develop towards its own goals by means of its own self-respect. Driessen makes this clear, with facts and imagery tempered with passion and humour."

Kelvin Kemm PhD, CEO, South Africa.

"I enjoyed your book very much. You cover a lot of ground in such a limited frame, but your arguments are coherent and you do not pull your punches."

David Knight, United Kingdom

"'Ideas and ideologies have consequences. Horrid ideas and ideologies have lethal consequences.' This is the central premise of the book *Eco-Imperialism - Green power, black death*. The lethal consequences of the idea that environmental values take precedence over the value of human lives is its central theme. And it documents these consequences in all their chilling detail.... What Paul Driessen documents in his book is that, by fanatically seeking to impose their agenda upon the whole of society, especially in the developing world, eco-imperialists are directly responsible for advocating policies that literally result in the deaths of countless millions of poor and desperate people about the globe.

Don Newman, Grassroot Institute of Hawaii, USA

"A developing country does not need First World ideological oppression. It needs to develop towards its own goals by means of its own self-respect. Driessen makes this clear, with facts and imagery tempered with passion and humour."

Kelvin Kemm PhD, CEO, South Africa

"After listening to you on the Dennis Prager Show, I am compelled to go out and purchase your book, one which should be read by every single non-White and low-income White in America - notably those who largely vote Democrat. The reason I make this statement is that eco-imperialism, although horrendous in Third-World countries, also has an impact here in the United States. Radical environmentalists in this country often oppose development. You may even hear some of these folks talk about 'Affordable Housing' - yet at the same time they lobby endlessly for regulations and restrictions that are often injurious to the majority of Black and Latino Americans. For example, due to high taxation and land-use restriction, the San Francisco Bay Area is one of the most prohibitive areas for minorities to reside - they simply cannot afford to live there. Because of their paranoid fear of sprawl, the elitist eco-imperialists virtually prevent upwardly-mobile people of color from improving their lot in life. Only we, the wealthy and privileged, they seem to insist, can live in 'nice' homes and safe neighborhoods. I look forward to reading your eye-opening account."

LaTonya Bethea, United States

"I had been reading your book during trips to the local Starbucks coffee shop where I live. I'm a regular customer and most of the employees there know me. After a few days of reading and drinking coffee, several of them (some who are pro-eco-group types) began to ask me questions about what I was reading (they thought from the picture it was a book about starvation, which in a way is accurate). There was one girl working there in particular who I thought was going to cry when I started giving her the FACTS about how many children die each year as a result of environmental policy in third world countries. During our talk, it became clear how much the Greenpeace-type-endorsed 'eco education' had brainwashed her. I also realized that the mission work my local Catholic church does is much more important than I realized in relation to bringing clean water and sewage systems to villages in South America. I've truly enjoyed your book and will continue to share my reading experience with other people."

Mark Allan, United States